**Fourth Edition**

# ITALIAN VERB DRILLS

## Paola Nanni-Tate

Mc
Graw
Hill
Education

New York   Chicago   San Francisco   Athens   London   Madrid
Mexico City   Milan   New Delhi   Singapore   Sydney   Toronto

1 2 3 4 5 6 7 8 9 10    LHS    22 21 20 19 18 17

ISBN      978-1-260-01064-0
MHID         1-260-01064-3

e-ISBN   978-1-260-01065-7
e-MHID      1-260-01065-1

Library of Congress Control Number: 2010925176

McGraw-Hill Education books are available at special quantity discounts to use as premiums and sales promotions or for use in corporate training programs. To contact a representative, please visit the Contact Us pages at www.mhprofessional.com.

**McGraw-Hill Education Language Lab App**

Review quizzes, flash cards, and a digital glossary are all available to support your study of this book. Go to www.mhlanguagelab.com to access the online version of the application, or to locate links to the mobile app for iOS and Android devices. More details about the features of the app are available on the inside front cover.

**Also in this series**

Nanni-Tate: *Italian Grammar Drills*
Stillman, Godor & Gordon: *Italian Vocabulary Drills*

# Table of Contents

# Introduction

*Italian Verb Drills* has been written for students of the Italian language who wish to take the time to master the structures and the conjugations of Italian verbs by learning the rules and doing the numerous exercises outlined in this book.

*Italian Verb Drills* covers verb tenses from the present indicative to the past subjunctive, and each tense is preceded by rules and examples to clairfiy its use. An answer key is supplied for the students to check their knowledge and progress, and the Indexes of Verbs list all the verbs covered in the book.

While *Italian Verb Drills* is not intended to cover "all" Italian verbs, it lists a large number of the verbs that are commonly used. This book will also serve as an example and a guide to learn other verbs that follow similar patterns.

For this latest edition, a helpful complement to this book is provided in the McGraw-Hill Education Language Lab app, available online and as a free mobile app. All verb lists that appear throughout this book are presented in flashcard format, providing a convenient means to memorization. The two verb indices are also included in a handy auto-fill glossary for quick reference. And for additional review, numerous interactive quizzes allow for helpful review on-the-go.

This book and its supporting digital resources should be an invaluable aid for students wishing to advance more quickly in their study of Italian. It has been inspired and encouraged by my husband Bob, and by all my students, especially those who have studied Italian with me for a long time. To all of them I give my thanks and I dedicate *Italian Verb Drills*.

Paola Nanni-Tate

# Chapter 1

## Overview of Italian Verbs

### 1. Verb Structure

All Italian verbs have four moods: (1) The *infinitive* expresses the action itself, with no reference to time or person. It is the form given in the dictionary. (2) The *indicative* expresses a thing as a fact, and it is the most commonly used mood. It has several tenses. (3) The *imperative* is used to give orders. It has one tense (present), and it is in the 2nd person (you) with singular and plural forms, and familiar and polite forms. The 1st person plural such as *andiamo* (let's go), *mangiamo* (let's eat) is also considered imperative. (4) The *subjunctive* expresses *possibility, hopes, feelings, wishes,* and it is almost always preceded by *che,* such as in *che io venga* (that I come).

Italian verbs have two numbers: singular and plural. They have three persons.

|            | Singular |         |             | Plural |          |          |
|------------|----------|---------|-------------|--------|----------|----------|
| 1st person | *io*     | *mangio* | I eat      | *noi*  | *mangiamo* | we eat   |
| 2nd person | *tu*     | *mangi*  | you eat    | *voi*  | *mangiate* | you eat  |
| 3rd person | *lui, lei* | *mangia* | he, she eats | *loro* | *mangiano* | they eat |

### 2. Subject Pronouns (Pronomi Personali)

In English, the subject pronouns are always used: *I, you, he, she, it, we, you, they.* In Italian, as a general rule, they are seldom needed since the endings of the verbs give the information about the person doing the action. Only in the 3rd person singular and the 3rd person plural could there be some confusion, so it is advisable to use *lui* (he), *lei* (she), *loro* (they). *It* can be translated with *esso* or *essa,* but nowadays these forms are not very commonly used.

In Italian, there are several ways to say **you**: In the singular, there are the informal *tu* and the formal *Lei,* which is used for both men and women and which is followed by the 3rd person singular of the verb. In the plural, *Loro* and the 3rd person plural of the verb are used when talking to more than one person formally and informally. *Voi* may also be used.

**Examples:**     Do you speak English?

**Singular:**
Informal     (Tu) parli inglese?
Formal       (Lei) parla inglese?

**Plural:**
Informal     (Voi) parlate inglese?
Formal       (Loro) parlano inglese?

## 3. Interrogative in Italian

Usually, there is no change in the word order in Italian when asking a question, only a change of intonation when speaking, and a question mark when writing. The **do, does, did** in English are not translated.

> **Example:**     Do you (informal) remember?     (Tu) ricordi?

## 4. Negative in Italian

The negative in Italian is formed by putting **non** in front of the verb. In compound tenses, **non** is placed in front of the auxiliary verb.

> **Examples:**     *Non mangio niente.*          I don't eat anything.
> *Non abbiamo parlato con lui.*     We didn't speak with him.

## 5. Infinitive and the Three Conjugations

All Italian verbs end in *-are, -ere,* or *-ire* in their infinitives.

> Verbs ending in *-are* (*mangiare,* to eat) are in the *1st conjugation.*
> Verbs ending in *-ere* (*vedere,* to see) are in the *2nd conjugation.*
> Verbs ending in *-ire* (*sentire,* to hear) are in the *3rd conjugation.*

# Verbs Ending in *-are*

## 6. Present Tense of *-are* Verbs

The *present indicative* of regular verbs in the 1st conjugation (*-are* verbs) is formed by adding *o, i, a, iamo, ate, ano* to the root of the verb. The root is obtained by dropping the *-are* ending from the infinitive.

**Parlare**                    **Mangiare**

Singular:

| | | | |
|---|---|---|---|
| io parl*o* | I speak | io mang*io* | I eat |
| tu parl*i* | you speak | tu mang*i* | you eat |
| lui parl*a* | he speaks | lui mang*ia* | he eats |
| lei parl*a* | she speaks | lei mang*ia* | she eats |

Plural:

| | | | |
|---|---|---|---|
| noi parl*iamo* | we speak | noi mang*iamo* | we eat |
| voi parl*ate* | you speak | voi mang*iate* | you eat |
| loro parl*ano* | they speak | loro mang*iano* | they eat |

**Note:** *Lei parla, lei mangia* are used for **she speaks, she eats,** or the formal, 2nd person singular, **you speak, you eat.**

Most verbs in the 1st conjugation are regular. (Some very common irregular ones are studied later in this chapter.) A few have some spelling differences.

   a. Verbs ending in *-care, -gare,* like *cercare* (to look for) and *pagare* (to pay), add *h* before endings with *i* or *e* to maintain the same sound of the root of the verb.

   **Examples:** *cerco* (I look for), *cerchi* (you look for).

   b. Verbs ending in *-ciare, -giare,* like *cominciare* (to begin) and *mangiare* (to eat), omit *i* before endings with *e* or *i.*

   **Examples:** *mangio* (I eat), *mangi* (you eat), not *mangii.*

   c. Verbs ending in *-iare* omit the *i* ending of the 2nd person singular of the present tense if the *i* is not in the accented syllable.

   **Examples:** For *studiare* (to study), forms are *studio, studi,* and not *studii.* For *avviare* (start) forms are *avvio, avvii,* and not *avvi!*

## 7. List of Common -are Verbs

Here are some common regular verbs ending in **-are.**

| | | | |
|---|---|---|---|
| **abitare** | to live | **litigare** | to quarrel |
| **aiutare** | to help | **mandare** | to send |
| **arrivare** | to arrive | **mostrare** | to show |
| **ascoltare** | to listen | **notare** | to notice |
| **aspettare** | to wait | **nuotare** | to swim |
| **ballare** | to dance | **pagare** | to pay |
| **cambiare** | to change | **pensare** | to think |
| **camminare** | to walk | **portare** | to bring |
| **cantare** | to sing | **pranzare** | to have lunch |
| **cenare** | to have supper | **provare** | to try |
| **cominciare** | to start | **raccontare** | to narrate |
| **contare** | to count | **rallentare** | to slow down |
| **dimenticare** | to forget | **regalare** | to give a gift |
| **domandare** | to ask | **ricordare** | to remember |
| **fermare** | to stop, to close | **riposare** | to rest |
| **giocare** | to play | **ritornare** | to return |
| **girare** | to turn | **saltare** | to jump |
| **guidare** | to drive | **spiegare** | to explain |
| **gustare** | to taste | **studiare** | to study |
| **imparare** | to learn | **suonare** | to play |
| **insegnare** | to teach | **tagliare** | to cut |
| **lasciare** | to leave, to let | **trovare** | to find |
| **lavare** | to wash | **viaggiare** | to travel |
| **lavorare** | to work | **volare** | to fly |

## 8. Practice

**Note:** All regular verbs ending in *-are* form the present indicative like the models in part 6.
Write the *present tense* of the verbs.

1. **cantare**       io _____ tu _____ lui, lei _____

   (to sing)        noi _____ voi _____ loro _____

2. **provare**       io _____ tu _____ lui, lei _____

   (to try)         noi _____ voi _____ loro _____

3. **lavorare**      io _____ tu _____ lui, lei _____

   (to work)        noi _____ voi _____ loro _____

4. **ricordare**     io _____ tu _____ lui, lei _____

   (to remember)    noi _____ voi _____ loro _____

5. **viaggiare**     io _____ tu _____ lui, lei _____

   (to travel)      noi _____ voi _____ loro _____

6. **volare**        io _____ tu _____ lui, lei _____

   (to fly)         noi _____ voi _____ loro _____

# 9. Practice

Write the *present tense* of the verbs in the person indicated by the pronoun.

**Io:**

| studiare | insegnare | viaggiare | saltare |
|---|---|---|---|
| _____ | _____ | _____ | _____ |

**Tu:**

| parlare | mangiare | trovare | ballare |
|---|---|---|---|
| _____ | _____ | _____ | _____ |

**Lui, Lei:**

| imparare | entrare | lavare | riposare |
|---|---|---|---|
| _____ | _____ | _____ | _____ |

**Noi:**

| comprare | arrivare | aiutare | tagliare |
|---|---|---|---|
| _____ | _____ | _____ | _____ |

**Voi:**

| parlare | imparare | aspettare | pensare |
|---|---|---|---|
| _____ | _____ | _____ | _____ |

**Loro:**

| spiegare | insegnare | contare | camminare |
|---|---|---|---|
| _____ | _____ | _____ | _____ |

## 10. Practice

Write the *present tense* of the verb in the person indicated by the pronoun.

1.  Noi (mangiare) _____

2.  Lui (imparare) _____

3.  Loro (comprare) _____

4.  Io (cantare) _____

5.  Tu (camminare) _____

6.  Voi (parlare) _____

7.  Noi (studiare) _____

8.  Lei (cambiare) _____

9.  Voi (pensare) _____

10. Lei (nuotare) _____

11. Io (giocare) _____

12. Noi (pranzare) _____

13. Voi (viaggiare) _____

14. Loro (ballare) _____

15. Lei (lavorare) _____

16. Noi (lavare) _____

17. Io (pensare) _____

18. Noi (imparare) _____

19. Io (ascoltare) _____

20. Lei (amare) _____

21. Voi (abitare) _____

22. Loro (pagare) _____

23. Tu (entrare) _____

24. Noi (ispezionare) _____

25. Lui (pensare) _____

26. Tu (mandare) _____

## 11. Practice

Rewrite in English in the right form and person.

1. Mangiamo _____

2. Imparo _____

3. Comprano _____

4. Canto _____

5. Cammini _____

6. Parlate _____

7. Studiamo _____

8. Cambio _____

9. Pensate _____

10. Nuoto _____

11. Gioco _____

12. Pranziamo _____

13. Viaggiate _____

14. Ballano _____

15. Lavora _____

16. Laviamo _____

17. Penso _____

18. Impariamo _____

19. Ascolto _____

20. Ama _____

21. Abitate _____

22. Pagano _____

23. Entri _____

24. Ispezioniamo _____

25. Pensa _____

26. Mandi _____

## 12. Practice

Rewrite in Italian.

1. I eat _____
2. You (s.) think _____
3. They learn _____
4. We sing _____
5. You (pl.) eat _____
6. He studies _____
7. She teaches _____
8. I learn _____
9. You (s.) work _____
10. They wash _____
11. She enters _____
12. We rest _____

13. You (s.) wait _____
14. They sing _____
15. I dance _____
16. We jump _____
17. I travel _____
18. He finds _____
19. We arrive _____
20. You (pl.) wait _____
21. She helps _____
22. I buy _____
23. She finds _____
24. We study _____

### Negative and Interrogative Forms

Rewrite in Italian.

1. I don't eat _____
2. You (s.) don't work _____
3. We don't remember _____
4. They don't work _____
5. She doesn't enter _____
6. I don't rest _____

7. Do you (s.) eat? _____
8. Do you (s.) work? _____
9. Do we remember? _____
10. Do they work? _____
11. Does she enter? _____
12. Do I rest? _____

## 13. Practice

Rewrite in English.

1. Parliamo _____

2. Salti _____

3. Pensa _____

4. Cantate _____

5. Suono _____

6. Mangiamo _____

7. Imparano _____

8. Trovi _____

9. Entriamo _____

10. Lavori _____

11. Insegniamo _____

12. Lavate _____

13. Riposo _____

14. Guarda _____

15. Camminiamo _____

16. Portate _____

17. Balli _____

18. Parlano _____

19. Viaggia _____

20. Aiutiamo _____

21. Ricordo _____

22. Dimentica _____

23. Non mangio _____

24. Non camminano _____

25. Non lavorate _____

26. Lavori? _____

## 14. Irregular Verbs Ending in -are

In the 1st conjugation, there are four irregular verbs:

| | | | |
|---|---|---|---|
| *stare* | to stay | *fare* | to make, to do |
| *dare* | to give | *andare* | to go |

The following are the conjugation of these irregular verbs:

### Stare

| | | |
|---|---|---|
| *io* | *sto* | I stay |
| *tu* | *stai* | you stay |
| *lui* | *sta* | he stays |
| *lei* | *sta* | she stays |
| *noi* | *stiamo* | we stay |
| *voi* | *state* | you stay |
| *loro* | *stanno* | they stay |

### Dare

| | | |
|---|---|---|
| *io* | *do* | I give |
| *tu* | *dai* | you give |
| *lui* | *dà* | he gives |
| *lei* | *dà* | she gives |
| *noi* | *diamo* | we give |
| *voi* | *date* | you give |
| *loro* | *danno* | they give |

### Fare

| | | |
|---|---|---|
| *io* | *faccio* | I make, I do |
| *tu* | *fai* | you make, you do |
| *lui* | *fa* | he makes, he does |
| *lei* | *fa* | she makes, she does |
| *noi* | *facciamo* | we make, we do |
| *voi* | *fate* | you make, you do |
| *loro* | *fanno* | they make, they do |

### Andare

| | | |
|---|---|---|
| *io* | *vado* | I go |
| *tu* | *vai* | you go |
| *lui* | *va* | he goes |
| *lei* | *va* | she goes |
| *noi* | *andiamo* | we go |
| *voi* | *andate* | you go |
| *loro* | *vanno* | they go |

## 15. Practice

Write the *present tense* of the verbs.

1. **dare**      io _____   tu _____   lui, lei _____

   (to give)    noi _____   voi _____   loro _____


2. **fare**      io _____   tu _____   lui, lei _____

   (to make, do)    noi _____   voi _____   loro _____


3. **stare**      io _____   tu _____   lui, lei _____

   (to stay)    noi _____   voi _____   loro _____


4. **andare**      io _____   tu _____   lui, lei _____

   (to go)    noi _____   voi _____   loro _____

# Chapter 2

## Verbs Ending in *-ere*

### 1. Present Tense of *-ere* Verbs

All the verbs ending in *-ere,* such as *temere* (to fear), belong to the 2nd conjugation. The *present* indicative of verbs in the 2nd conjugation is formed by adding *o, i, e, iamo, ete, ono* to the root of the verb.

| **Vedere** | | To see | **Scrivere** | | To write |
|---|---|---|---|---|---|
| io | ved*o* | I see | io | scriv*o* | I write |
| tu | ved*i* | you see | tu | scriv*i* | you write |
| lui | ved*e* | he sees | lui | scriv*e* | he writes |
| lei | ved*e* | she sees | lei | scriv*e* | she writes |
| noi | ved*iamo* | we see | noi | scriv*iamo* | we write |
| voi | ved*ete* | you see | voi | scriv*ete* | you write |
| loro | ved*ono* | they see | loro | scriv*ono* | they write |

In the present tense of some *-ere* verbs, the pronunciation changes, but the spelling of the root and the endings stay the same. In verbs ending in *-cere* and *-gere,* such as *vincere* (to win) and *leggere* (to read), the pronunciation changes to a hard sound when the *o* or *a* follows *c* or *g.*

**Examples:**    Vin*co,* vinci, vince, vinciamo, vincete, vin*cono*
Legg*o,* leggi, legge, leggiamo, leggete, legg*ono*

## 2. List of Common *-ere* Verbs

Here are some common verbs ending in *-ere.*

| | | | |
|---|---|---|---|
| **accadere** | to happen | **esistere** | to exist |
| **accedere** | to access | **godere** | to enjoy |
| **accendere** | to turn on | **includere** | to include |
| **apprendere** | to learn | **insistere** | to insist |
| **assistere** | to assist | **leggere** | to read |
| **assolvere** | to absolve | **mettere** | to put |
| **assumere** | to assume, hire | **nascondere** | to hide |
| **attendere** | to wait for, attend | **perdere** | to lose |
| **cadere** | to fall | **permettere** | to allow |
| **cedere** | to yield | **piangere** | to cry |
| **chiedere** | to ask | **prendere** | to take |
| **chiudere** | to close | **pretendere** | to pretend |
| **comprendere** | to comprehend | **promettere** | to promise |
| **concludere** | to conclude | **promuovere** | to promote |
| **condividere** | to share | **ridere** | to laugh |
| **confondere** | to confuse | **risolvere** | to resolve |
| **conoscere** | to know | **rispondere** | to answer |
| **consistere** | to consist | **rompere** | to break |
| **convincere** | to convince | **scendere** | to descend |
| **correggere** | to correct | **scrivere** | to write |
| **correre** | to run | **sorridere** | to smile |
| **credere** | to believe | **spingere** | to push |
| **crescere** | to grow | **succedere** | to happen |
| **decidere** | to decide | **temere** | to fear |
| **difendere** | to defend | **trasmettere** | to broadcast |
| **discutere** | to discuss | **vedere** | to see |
| **distinguere** | to distinguish | **vincere** | to win |
| **dividere** | to divide | **vivere** | to live |

**Note:** Some of the above verbs are irregular in other forms, but they all form the *present indicative* with the regular endings.

## 3. Practice

**Note:** Most verbs in *-ere* form the present tense like the above models in part 1. Write the *present tense* of the verbs.

1. **dividere**     io _____     tu _____     lui, lei _____

   (to divide)     noi _____     voi _____     loro_____


2. **chiudere**     io _____     tu _____     lui, lei _____

   (to close)     noi _____     voi _____     loro_____


3. **mettere**     io _____     tu _____     lui, lei _____

   (to put)     noi _____     voi _____     loro_____


4. **convincere**     io _____     tu _____     lui, lei _____

   (to convince)     noi _____     voi _____     loro_____


5. **spingere**     io _____     tu _____     lui, lei _____

   (to push)     noi _____     voi _____     loro_____


6. **perdere**     io _____     tu _____     lui, lei _____

   (to lose)     noi _____     voi _____     loro_____

# 4. Practice

Write the present tense of the verbs in the person indicated.

**Io:**

| apprendere | attendere | chiedere | chiudere |
|---|---|---|---|
| _____ | _____ | _____ | _____ |

**Tu:**

| cadere | confondere | dividere | crescere |
|---|---|---|---|
| _____ | _____ | _____ | _____ |

**Lui, Lei:**

| decidere | difendere | discutere | concludere |
|---|---|---|---|
| _____ | _____ | _____ | _____ |

**Noi:**

| apprendere | attendere | insistere | esistere |
|---|---|---|---|
| _____ | _____ | _____ | _____ |

**Voi:**

| cadere | ridere | rispondere | nascondere |
|---|---|---|---|
| _____ | _____ | _____ | _____ |

**Loro:**

| perdere | piangere | insistere | promettere |
|---|---|---|---|
| _____ | _____ | _____ | _____ |

## 5. Practice

Rewrite in Italian.

1. I fear _____
2. You (s.) wait for _____
3. He falls _____
4. We ask _____
5. You (s.) assist _____
6. He closes _____
7. They confuse _____
8. You (s.) know _____
9. They decide _____
10. He defends _____
11. She discusses _____
12. We decide _____
13. He asks _____

14. You (s.) enjoy _____
15. I conclude _____
16. She insists _____
17. We put _____
18. He loses _____
19. I promise _____
20. We promise _____
21. We cry _____
22. They answer _____
23. I see _____
24. She sees _____
25. I write _____
26. I cry _____

### Negative and Interrogative Forms

Rewrite in Italian.

1. I don't assist _____
2. You don't (s.) wait for _____
3. We don't ask _____
4. They don't divide _____
5. She doesn't close _____
6. He doesn't cry _____

7. Do you (s.) assist? _____
8. Do you (s.) wait for? _____
9. Do you (s.) ask? _____
10. Do they divide? _____
11. Do you (s.) close? _____
12. Do you (s.) cry? _____

## 6. Practice

Rewrite in English.

1.  Apprendiamo_____
2.  Teme_____
3.  Assumiamo_____
4.  Attendono_____
5.  Cado_____
6.  Credete_____
7.  Chiede_____
8.  Chiudono_____
9.  Correggi_____
10. Concludete_____
11. Condividono_____
12. Confondono_____
13. Conosci_____
14. Conoscono_____
15. Cuocete_____
16. Cuoce_____
17. Decido_____
18. Difendete_____
19. Discutiamo_____
20. Includiamo_____
21. Insiste_____
22. Perdete_____
23. Perdono_____
24. Piangono_____
25. Pretende_____
26. Rispondi_____
27. Vedo_____
28. Vinci_____
29. Conosce_____
30. Vincono_____
31. Ridete_____
32. Rompono_____
33. Non rimango_____
34. Non permettono_____
35. Non leggiamo_____
36. Leggete?_____
37. Leggi?_____
38. Vediamo?_____
39. Scrive?_____
40. Temono?_____
41. Non vedete?_____
42. Non leggi?_____
43. Non scrivono?_____
44. Non scriviamo?_____

# 7. Irregular Verbs Ending in -ere

In the 2nd conjugation, there are many irregular verbs. Here are some of the most common.

| **Bere** | To drink | | **Cogliere** | To gather |
|---|---|---|---|---|
| io bevo | I drink | | io colgo | I gather |
| tu bevi | you drink | | tu cogli | you gather |
| lui beve | he drinks | | lui coglie | he gathers |
| lei beve | she drinks | | lei coglie | she gathers |
| noi beviamo | we drink | | noi cogliamo | we gather |
| voi bevete | you drink | | voi cogliete | you gather |
| loro bevono | they drink | | loro colgono | they gather |

| **Dovere** | Must, to have to | | **Porre** | To put |
|---|---|---|---|---|
| io devo | I must/have to | | io pongo | I put |
| tu devi | you must/have to | | tu poni | you put |
| lui deve | he must/has to | | lui pone | he puts |
| lei deve | she must/has to | | lei pone | she puts |
| noi dobbiamo | we must/have to | | noi poniamo | we put |
| voi dovete | you must/have to | | voi ponete | you put |
| loro devono | thcy must/have to | | loro pongono | they put |

| **Potere** | To be able | | **Rimanere** | To stay |
|---|---|---|---|---|
| io posso | I am able | | io rimango | I stay |
| tu puoi | you are able | | tu rimani | you stay |
| lui può | he is able | | lui rimane | he stays |
| lei può | she is able | | lei rimane | she stays |
| noi possiamo | we are able | | noi rimaniamo | we stay |
| voi potete | you are able | | voi rimanete | you stay |
| loro possono | they are able | | loro rimangono | they stay |

| **Sapere** | To know | | **Scegliere** | To choose |
|---|---|---|---|---|
| io so | I know | | io scelgo | I choose |
| tu sai | you know | | tu scegli | you choose |
| lui sa | he knows | | lui sceglie | he chooses |
| lei sa | she knows | | lei sceglie | she chooses |
| noi sappiamo | we know | | noi scegliamo | we choose |
| voi sapete | you know | | voi scegliete | you choose |
| loro sanno | they know | | loro scelgono | they choose |

| **Sedere** | To sit | | **Spegnere** | To turn off |
|---|---|---|---|---|
| io siedo | I sit | | io spengo | I turn off |
| tu siedi | you sit | | tu spegni | you turn off |
| lui siede | he sits | | lui spegne | he turns off |
| lei siede | she sits | | lei spegne | she turns off |
| noi sediamo | we sit | | noi spegniamo | we turn off |
| voi sedete | you sit | | voi spegnete | you turn off |
| loro siedono | they sit | | loro spengono | they turn off |

| Tenere | To keep | Volere | To want |
|--------|---------|--------|---------|
| io tengo | I keep | io voglio | I want |
| tu tieni | you keep | tu vuoi | you want |
| lui tiene | he keeps | lui vuole | he wants |
| lei tiene | she keeps | lei vuole | she wants |
| noi teniamo | we keep | noi vogliamo | we want |
| voi tenete | you keep | voi volete | you want |
| loro tengono | they keep | loro vogliono | they want |

## 8. Practice

Write the *present tense* of the verbs.

1. **dovere**      io _____   tu _____   lui, lei _____

   (must)       noi _____   voi _____   loro _____


2. **scegliere**   io _____   tu _____   lui, lei _____

   (to choose)  noi _____   voi _____   loro _____


3. **potere**      io _____   tu _____   lui, lei _____

   (to be able) noi _____   voi _____   loro _____


4. **sapere**      io _____   tu _____   lui, lei _____

   (to know)    noi _____   voi _____   loro _____


5. **tenere**      io _____   tu _____   lui, lei _____

   (to keep)    noi _____   voi _____   loro _____


6. **volere**      io _____   tu _____   lui, lei _____

   (to want)    noi _____   voi _____   loro _____

# Verbs Ending in *-ire*

## 9. Present Indicative of *-ire* Verbs

All the verbs ending in *ire,* such as *partire* (to depart, to leave) and *dormire* (to sleep), belong to the 3rd conjugation.

The *present indicative* of verbs in the 3rd conjugation is formed by adding *o, i, e, iamo, ite, ono* to the root of the verb. Many verbs of the 3rd conjugation insert *isc* between the root and the endings of the present tense.

| **Dormire** | To sleep | **Finire** | To finish |
|---|---|---|---|
| io   dorm*o* | I sleep | io   fin*isco* | I finish |
| tu   dorm*i* | you sleep | tu   fin*isci* | you finish |
| lui  dorm*e* | he sleeps | lui  fin*isce* | he finishes |
| lei  dorm*e* | she sleeps | lei  fin*isce* | she finishes |
| noi  dorm*iamo* | we sleep | noi  fin*iamo* | we finish |
| voi  dorm*ite* | you sleep | voi  fin*ite* | you finish |
| loro dorm*ono* | they sleep | loro fin*iscono* | they finish |

The following *-ire* verbs do not insert *isc* when conjugated:

| | | | |
|---|---|---|---|
| **acconsentire** | to agree | **fuggire** | to escape |
| **applaudire** | to applaud | **inghiottire** | to swallow |
| **aprire** | to open | **inseguire** | to follow |
| **assentire** | to agree, to consent | **investire** | to invest |
| **avvertire** | to announce | **mentire** | to lie |
| **bollire** | to boil | **offrire** | to offer |
| **conseguire** | to result | **partire** | to leave, depart |
| **consentire** | to agree | **seguire** | to follow |
| **convertire** | to convert | **sentire** | to hear |
| **coprire** | to cover | **servire** | to serve |
| **divertire** | to enjoy | **soffrire** | to suffer |
| **eseguire** | to do | **vestire** | to dress |

The following *-ire* verbs insert *isc* in the present tense of the indicative.

| | | | |
|---|---|---|---|
| **aderire** | to adhere | **guarire** | to heal |
| **attribuire** | to attribute | **impazzire** | to go mad |
| **benedire** | to bless | **inserire** | to insert |
| **capire** | to understand | **istruire** | to instruct |
| **colpire** | to hit | **preferire** | to prefer |
| **costruire** | to build | **pulire** | to clean |
| **definire** | to define | **punire** | to punish |
| **digerire** | to digest | **restituire** | to return |
| **dimagrire** | to lose weight | **riunire** | to meet |
| **esaurire** | to exhaust | **sostituire** | to substitute |
| **esibire** | to exhibit | **spedire** | to send |
| **fallire** | to fail | **stabilire** | to establish |
| **ferire** | to wound | **suggerire** | to suggest |
| **finire** | to finish | **tradire** | to betray |
| **garantire** | to guarantee | **trasferire** | to transfer |
| **gestire** | to manage | **ubbidire** | to obey |

**Note:** Some of the above verbs are irregular, but they all form the present indicative with regular endings.

## 10. Practice

Most verbs ending in *-ire* form the present indicative like the models on page 21.
Write the *present tense* of the verbs.

1.  **avvertire**      io _____   tu _____   lui, lei _____

    (to notify)      noi _____   voi _____   loro _____


2.  **bollire**       io _____   tu _____   lui, lei _____

    (to boil)       noi _____   voi _____   loro _____


3.  **sentire**       io _____   tu _____   lui, lei _____

    (to hear)       noi _____   voi _____   loro _____


4.  **capire**        io _____   tu _____   lui, lei _____

    (to understand)   noi _____   voi _____   loro _____


5.  **preferire**     io _____   tu _____   lui, lei _____

    (to prefer)      noi _____   voi _____   loro _____

# 11. Practice

Write the *present tense* of the following *-ire* verbs in the indicated person.

**Io:**

| aprire | capire | offrire | finire |
|--------|--------|---------|--------|
| _____ | _____ | _____ | _____ |

**Tu:**

| dormire | avvertire | bollire | sentire |
|---------|-----------|---------|---------|
| _____ | _____ | _____ | _____ |

**Lui, Lei:**

| preferire | partire | vestire | spedire |
|-----------|---------|---------|---------|
| _____ | _____ | _____ | _____ |

**Noi:**

| servire | vestire | aprire | capire |
|---------|---------|--------|--------|
| _____ | _____ | _____ | _____ |

**Voi:**

| avvertire | seguire | costruire | istruire |
|-----------|---------|-----------|----------|
| _____ | _____ | _____ | _____ |

**Loro:**

| sentire | inseguire | investire | partire |
|---------|-----------|-----------|---------|
| _____ | _____ | _____ | _____ |

## 12. Practice

Rewrite in Italian.

1. I prefer_____
2. You (s.) consent_____
3. He covers_____
4. We enjoy_____
5. They escape_____
6. He understands_____
7. He follows_____
8. You (s.) lie_____
9. I hear_____
10. We suffer_____
11. They open_____
12. He finishes_____

13. You (s.) applaud_____
14. He converts_____
15. I applaud_____
16. He sleeps_____
17. I swallow_____
18. You (pl.) leave_____
19. They serve_____
20. I sleep_____
21. She prefers_____
22. I understand_____
23. We prefer_____
24. I build_____

### Negative and Interrogative Forms

Rewrite in Italian.

1. I don't finish_____
2. He doesn't understand_____
3. They don't instruct_____
4. You (s.) don't hear_____
5. I don't sleep_____
6. We don't applaud_____
7. We don't leave_____
8. I don't suffer_____

9. Do we build?_____
10. Does he hear?_____
11. Do they understand?_____
12. Do they hear?_____
13. Does he sleep?_____
14. Do you consent?_____
15. Does she finish?_____
16. Do we depart?_____

# 13. Practice

Rewrite in English.

1. Acconsenti_____
2. Applaudono_____
3. Apre_____
4. Aprono_____
5. Avvertiamo_____
6. Bolle_____
7. Capisco_____
8. Consentite_____
9. Convertono_____
10. Copro_____
11. Costruisce_____
12. Offre_____
13. Divertiamo_____
14. Dormite_____
15. Seguono_____
16. Finiamo_____
17. Fugge_____

18. Guarisci_____
19. Garantiscono_____
20. Inghiotti_____
21. Inseguono_____
22. Istruisce_____
23. Preferiscono_____
24. Seguite_____
25. Pulite_____
26. Puniscono_____
27. Colpisce_____
28. Servo_____
29. Soffre_____
30. Sostituisco_____
31. Spediamo_____
32. Sostituiscono_____
33. Suggeriamo_____
34. Trasferiscono_____

## Negative and Interrogative Forms

1. Non dormiamo _____
2. Non soffre_____
3. Non capiamo_____
4. Non istruisce_____
5. Non apri _____

6. Acconsenti?_____
7. Partono? _____
8. Dormi? _____
9. Capisci?_____
10. Pulite? _____

## 14. Irregular Verb Endings in -ire

In the 3rd conjugation, there are many irregular verbs. The most common are:

| | | | |
|---|---|---|---|
| *dire* | to tell, say | *udire* | to hear |
| *morire* | to die | *uscire* | to go out, exit |
| *salire* | to go up, ascend | *venire* | to come |

The following are the conjugations of the present indicative of the above verbs:

### Dire — To tell, say

| | | |
|---|---|---|
| *io* | *dico* | I tell, say |
| *tu* | *dici* | you tell, say |
| *lui* | *dice* | he tells, says |
| *lei* | *dice* | she tells, says |
| *noi* | *diciamo* | we tell, say |
| *voi* | *dite* | you tell, say |
| *loro* | *dicono* | they tell, say |

### Morire — To die

| | | |
|---|---|---|
| *io* | *muoio* | I die |
| *tu* | *muori* | you die |
| *lui* | *muore* | he dies |
| *lei* | *muore* | she dies |
| *noi* | *moriamo* | we die |
| *voi* | *morite* | you die |
| *loro* | *muoiono* | they die |

### Salire — To climb

| | | |
|---|---|---|
| *io* | *salgo* | I climb |
| *tu* | *sali* | you climb |
| *lui* | *sale* | he climbs |
| *lei* | *sale* | she climbs |
| *noi* | *saliamo* | we climb |
| *voi* | *salite* | you climb |
| *loro* | *salgono* | they climb |

### Udire — To hear

| | | |
|---|---|---|
| *io* | *odo* | I hear |
| *tu* | *odi* | you hear |
| *lui* | *ode* | he hears |
| *lei* | *ode* | she hears |
| *noi* | *udiamo* | we hear |
| *voi* | *udite* | you hear |
| *loro* | *odono* | they hear |

### Uscire — To go out

| | | |
|---|---|---|
| *io* | *esco* | I go out |
| *tu* | *esci* | you go out |
| *lui* | *esce* | he goes out |
| *lei* | *esce* | she goes out |
| *noi* | *usciamo* | we go out |
| *voi* | *uscite* | you go out |
| *loro* | *escono* | they go out |

### Venire — To come

| | | |
|---|---|---|
| *io* | *vengo* | I come |
| *tu* | *vieni* | you come |
| *lui* | *viene* | he comes |
| *lei* | *viene* | she comes |
| *noi* | *veniamo* | we come |
| *voi* | *venite* | you come |
| *loro* | *vengono* | they come |

## 15. Practice

Write the *present tense* of the verbs.

1. **venire**      io _____  tu _____  lui, lei _____

   (to come)     noi _____  voi _____  loro _____

2. **dire**        io _____  tu _____  lui, lei _____

   (to say)      noi _____  voi _____  loro _____

3. **uscire**      io _____  tu _____  lui, lei _____

   (to go out)   noi _____  voi _____  loro _____

## 16. Practice

Rewrite in Italian.

1. you (s.) say _____

2. they go out _____

3. we come _____

4. they die _____

5. I climb _____

6. she says _____

7. I go out _____

8. they come _____

9. they climb _____

10. we go out _____

11. you (pl.) climb _____

12. he dies _____

13. you (s.) hear _____

14. they say _____

15. we hear _____

16. you (pl.) say _____

# Chapter 3

## Imperative

### 1. Uses of the Imperative: Familiar Forms

The *imperative* is for commands and orders. It is used in the *tu* and *voi* forms, *tu* for singular, familiar and *voi* for the plural, familiar. The forms are similar to the present tense except for the *tu* form of the 1st conjugation, which ends in *a* instead of *i.*

> Examples:   *parla* (speak) instead of *parli, mangia* (eat), instead of *mangi*

The 1st person plural of the present tense can be used in the imperative, but it is mostly a suggestion and an urgent request rather than a command.

> Examples:   *scriviamo* (let's write), *mangiamo* (let's eat), *andiamo* (let's go)

The negative *imperative* for *tu* is formed by *non* + the infinitive of the verb.

> Example:   *Non parlare* (don't speak), *non andare* (don't go)

For the 2nd person plural or *voi, non* is put in front of the *imperative* form.

> Example:   *Non parlate* (don't speak), *non scrivete* (don't write)

> Note: The formal forms of the imperative are introduced on page 32.

### 2. Familiar Imperative Forms

| | | |
|---|---|---|
| *parla* (speak) | *scrivi* (write) | *pulisci* (clean) |
| *parliamo* (let's speak) | *scriviamo* (let's write) | *puliamo* (let's clean) |
| *parlate* (speak pl.) | *scrivete* (write pl.) | *pulite* (clean pl.) |

Negative:

| | | |
|---|---|---|
| *non parlare* (don't speak) | *non scrivere* (don't write) | *non pulire* (don't clean) |
| *non parlate* (don't speak pl.) | *non scrivete* (don't write pl.) | *non pulite* (don't clean pl.) |

# 3. Practice

Rewrite in Italian in the imperative. Use the singular form unless plural (pl.) is indicated.

1. Speak _____

2. Sing _____

3. Go (pl.) _____

4. Don't go _____

5. Let's go _____

6. Don't eat (pl.) _____

7. Let's finish _____

8. Don't play (pl.) _____

9. Play _____

10. Look _____

11. Listen _____

12. Don't leave _____

13. Let's leave _____

14. Play (pl.) _____

15. Let's play _____

16. Go out _____

17. Don't go out (pl.) _____

18. Play _____

19. Don't play _____

20. Eat (pl.) _____

21. Write _____

22. Don't write _____

23. Let's write _____

24. Close _____

25. Don't close _____

26. Let's close _____

27. Sleep _____

28. Sleep (pl.) _____

29. Drink _____

30. Drink (pl.) _____

31. Read _____

32. Let's read _____

33. Don't read _____

34. Don't read (pl.) _____

# 4. Practice

Rewrite in English.

1. Parlate _____
2. Canta _____
3. Non cantare _____
4. Ascolta _____
5. Ascoltate _____
6. Andiamo _____
7. Parla _____
8. Non parlare _____
9. Giochiamo _____
10. Non giocate _____
11. Uscite _____
12. Non uscire _____
13. Mangia _____
14. Mangiamo _____
15. Chiudi _____
16. Chiedete _____
17. Pensa _____
18. Non pensate _____
19. Suggerisci _____
20. Parti _____
21. Mettete _____
22. Non mettere _____
23. Spera _____
24. Entrate _____
25. Studia _____
26. Non studiare _____
27. Non partite _____
28. Canta _____
29. Cantiamo _____
30. Spingi _____
31. Non spingere _____
32. Prendete _____

# 5. Irregular Imperative

There are a few irregular verbs with an irregular *tu* form of the imperative. They are:

|  | Imperative | |
|---|---|---|
| *andare* (to go) | *và* or *vai* | |
| *avere* (to have) | *abbi* | *abbiate* (irregular plural) |
| *dare* (to give) | *dà* or *dai* | |
| *dire* (to say, to tell) | *dì* | |
| *essere* (to be) | *sii* | *siate* (irregular plural) |
| *stare* (to stay) | *stà* or *stai* | |

# 6. The *Lei* and *Loro* Forms of the Imperative

The *imperative* for *Lei* and *Loro* is the same as the 3rd person of the present subjunctive (chapter 7). These forms are the formal polite forms.

|     | *Parlare* | *Scrivere* | *Sentire* | *Finire* |
|-----|-----------|------------|-----------|----------|
| Lei | *parli*   | scriva     | senta     | finisca  |
| Loro | *parlino* | scrivano   | sentano   | finiscano |

**Examples:**

*Singular:*

| | |
|---|---|
| *Parli* con la signora! | Speak with the lady! |
| *Scriva* subito la lettera! | Write the letter immediately! |
| *Senta* la radio! | Listen to the radio! |
| *Finisca* di mangiare! | Finish eating! |

*Plural:*

| | |
|---|---|
| *Parlino* con la signora! | Speak with the lady! |
| *Scrivano* subito! | Write immediately! |
| *Sentano* la radio! | Listen to the radio! |
| *Finiscano* di mangiare! | Finish eating! |

Many of the common verbs have irregular command forms for the polite singular and plural. Following are the most common.

|                      | **Singular** | **Plural** |
|----------------------|--------------|------------|
| *andare* (to go)     | *vada*       | *vadano*   |
| *bere* (to drink)    | *beva*       | *bevano*   |
| *dare* (to give)     | *dia*        | *diano*    |
| *dire* (to tell, say) | *dica*      | *dicano*   |
| *fare* (to do, to make) | *faccia*  | *facciano* |
| *stare* (to stay)    | *stia*       | *stiano*   |
| *temere* (to fear)   | *tema*       | *temano*   |
| *venire* (to come)   | *venga*      | *vengano*  |

The *negative imperative* formal is formed by placing *non* before the affirmative.

| **Examples:** | *Non parli!* | Don't speak! |
|---|---|---|
| | *Non scrivano!* | Don't write! |

Object and reflexive pronouns *always precede* the *Lei* and *Loro* forms.

| **Examples:** | *Mi scriva!* | Write me! |
|---|---|---|
| | *Non mi scriva!* | Don't write to me! |

## 7. Practice

Rewrite in English, using the *polite forms* of the *imperative* singular and plural as indicated.

1. Wait (s.) _____

2. Wait (pl.)_____

3. Pay (s.) _____

4. Pay (pl.)_____

5. Eat (s.) _____

6. Answer (pl.) _____

7. Finish (s.) _____

8. Look (pl.) _____

9. Come (s.) _____

10. Eat (pl.)_____

11. Answer (s.)_____

12. Finish (pl.)_____

13. Come (pl.)_____

14. Go out (s.) _____

15. Leave (pl.)_____

16. Tell me (s.)_____

17. Think (s.) _____

18. Go out (pl.)_____

19. Walk (s.)_____

20. Sing (pl.)_____

21. Read (pl.) _____

22. Smile (s.) _____

# Future

## 8. Forms of the Future

The *future tense* in Italian consists of a single verb while in English it consists of the auxiliary *shall* or *will* and the infinitive of the verb. The future of regular verbs is formed by putting the future endings on the infinitive of the verb without the final *e*. In the 1st conjugation, the *a* of the infinitive ending changes to *e* in the future.

**Examples:** *Parlare* (to speak)    *Scrivere* (to write)    *Sentire* (to hear)
              *Parlerò* (I'll speak)   *Scriverò* (I'll write)   *Sentirò* (I'll hear)

| Parlare | Scrivere | Sentire |
|---|---|---|
| io parler*ò* | io scriver*ò* | io sentir*ò* |
| tu parler*ai* | tu scriver*ai* | tu sentir*ai* |
| lui parler*à* | lui scriver*à* | lui sentir*à* |
| lei parler*à* | lei scriver*à* | lei sentir*à* |
| noi parler*emo* | noi scriver*emo* | noi sentir*emo* |
| voi parler*ete* | voi scriver*ete* | voi sentir*ete* |
| loro parler*anno* | loro scriver*anno* | loro sentir*anno* |

**Note:** The 1st and the 3rd persons singular have an accent on the ending. This means that the last syllable must be stressed.

Verbs ending in *-care* and *-gare* add an *h* to the future tense stem to keep the hard *c* and *g* sounds.

**Examples:** *Pagare* (to pay)      *Io pagherò* (I'll pay)
              *Giocare* (to play)    *Io giocherò* (I'll play)

Verbs ending in *-ciare* and *-giare* drop the *i* in the future tense stem.

**Examples:** *Cominciare* (to begin)   *Io comincerò* (I'll begin)
              *Mangiare* (to eat)     *Io mangerò* (I'll eat)

Here are some verbs that have irregular stems in the future. The endings are the same as the regular future endings.

| Infinitive | Future Stem | Conjugation |
|---|---|---|
| **andare** (to go) | *andr* | andrò, andrai, andrà, etc. |
| **avere** (to have) | *avr* | avrò, avrai, avrà, etc. |
| **bere** (to drink) | *berr* | berrò, berrai, berrà, etc. |
| **cadere** (to fall) | *cadr* | cadrò, cadrai, cadrà, etc. |
| **dare** (to give) | *dar* | darò, darai, darà, etc. |
| **essere** (to be) | *sar* | sarò, sarai, sarà, etc. |
| **fare** (to make) | *far* | farò, farai, farà, etc. |
| **porre** (to put) | *porr* | porrò, porrai, porrà, etc. |
| **sapere** (to know) | *sapr* | saprò, saprai, saprà, etc. |
| **tenere** (to hold) | *terr* | terrò, terrai, terrà, etc. |
| **vedere** (to see) | *vedr* | vedrò, vedrai, vedrà, etc. |
| **venire** (to come) | *verr* | verrò, verrai, verrà, etc. |

## 9. Practice

Write the *future* tense of the verbs.

1. **vedere**     io _____     tu _____     lui, lei _____
   (to see)       noi _____     voi _____     loro _____

2. **andare**     io _____     tu _____     lui, lei _____
   (to go)        noi _____     voi _____     loro _____

3. **capire**     io _____     tu _____     lui, lei _____
   (to understand) noi _____     voi _____     loro _____

4. **aiutare**    io _____     tu _____     lui, lei _____
   (to help)      noi _____     voi _____     loro _____

# 10. Practice

Write the verbs in the *future* tense in the person indicated.

**Io:**

parlare                          vedere                          pulire

_____      _____      _____


**Tu:**

viaggiare                      permettere                  capire

_____      _____      _____


**Lui, Lei:**

trovare                          sapere                          sentire

_____      _____      _____


**Noi:**

guardare                      bere                              finire

_____      _____      _____


**Voi:**

lavorare                        avere                            partire

_____      _____      _____


**Loro:**

andare                          essere                          sentire

_____      _____      _____

# 11. Practice

Rewrite in English.

1. Capirò _____
2. Lavorerò _____
3. Leggerai _____
4. Canterà _____
5. Sentirete _____
6. Pianterai _____
7. Ascolterò _____
8. Pianterete _____
9. Vedremo _____
10. Risponderanno _____
11. Pagherò _____
12. Giocheremo _____
13. Penserai _____
14. Vedrete _____
15. Sentirai _____
16. Deciderò _____
17. Piangeremo _____
18. Vincerà _____
19. Discuterete _____
20. Andremo _____
21. Studierò _____
22. Penserete _____
23. Scriverai _____
24. Cuocerò _____
25. Finirò _____
26. Giocheremo _____
27. Staremo _____
28. Farai _____
29. Darete _____
30. Partirai _____
31. Direte _____
32. Dormiremo _____
33. Inseguirai _____
34. Verremo _____
35. Bollirò _____
36. Applaudiranno _____
37. Aprirà _____
38. Saliremo _____

## Negative Future Forms

Rewrite in English.

1. Non mangerò _____
2. Non andremo _____
3. Non farà _____
4. Non canteremo _____
5. Non capirà _____
6. Non finirete _____

## 12. Practice

Rewrite in Italian.

1. I'll attend _____
2. He'll fall _____
3. We'll write _____
4. They'll think _____
5. We'll understand _____
6. I'll close _____
7. You'll (s.) speak _____
8. We'll play _____
9. They'll travel _____
10. I'll put _____
11. We'll do _____
12. He'll find _____
13. We'll find _____
14. I'll listen _____
15. We'll learn _____
16. I'll eat _____
17. We'll go _____
18. They'll make _____
19. I'll stay _____
20. I'll buy _____

21. They'll come _____
22. I'll come _____
23. We'll look _____
24. We'll say _____
25. He'll tell _____
26. They'll sing _____
27. We'll cry _____
28. I'll plant _____
29. We'll go out _____
30. They'll climb _____
31. You'll (pl.) go _____
32. We'll follow _____
33. He'll insist _____
34. She'll see _____
35. We'll answer _____
36. I'll pay _____
37. We'll vote _____
38. I'll decide _____
39. We'll drink _____
40. We'll hear _____

### Negative Future Forms

Rewrite in Italian.

1. I won't eat _____
2. He won't listen _____

3. We won't drink _____
4. They won't eat _____

# Chapter 4

## Imperfect

### 1. Uses of the Imperfect

This is a very easy tense to learn, but not so easy to use.

In Italian, the *imperfect* is always used to refer to an action in the past that is continuing while another takes place.

| | | |
|---|---|---|
| **Example:** | Mentre *parlavo,* tu arrivasti. | While I *was speaking,* you came. |

The *imperfect tense* in Italian expresses the English *used to.*

| | | |
|---|---|---|
| **Example:** | *Parlavo.* | I used to speak. |

With verbs of *thinking, believing,* and *feeling,* the imperfect is generally used rather than the other past forms—the *past definite (passato remoto)* or the *present perfect (passato prossimo),* found in future lessons.

| | | |
|---|---|---|
| **Examples:** | *Volevo* scrivere. | I wanted to write. |
| | Mi *sentivo* male. | I felt bad. |

The *imperfect* is used to describe actions or conditions that lasted for an indefinite period of time in the past. In English, this is the same as the form expressed by *was* and the *ing* form of the verb.

| | | |
|---|---|---|
| **Examples:** | *Leggevo* il giornale. | I *was reading* the newspaper. |
| | *Guardavo* la televisione. | I *was watching* television. |

The *Imperfect* is used to express habitual action in the past, and it is usually preceded or followed by words such as *di solito, qualche volta, spesso, sempre.*

| | | |
|---|---|---|
| **Examples:** | *Studiava sempre* con la sua amica. | She used to always study with her friend. |
| | Di solito, *guardavo* la televisione. | Usually, I would watch TV. |

The *imperfect* tense is used to describe time, age, weather, in the past.

| | | |
|---|---|---|
| **Example:** | *Faceva* bel tempo/brutto tempo. | The weather was nice/bad. |

## 2. Forms of the Imperfect

The *imperfect* is formed by adding the same endings to all three conjugations. The only difference among the conjugations is the typical vowel of the infinitive.

| | |
|---|---|
| parlare—parl*avo* | (To speak—I used to speak) |
| credere—cred*evo* | (To believe—I used to believe) |
| finire—fin*ivo* | (To finish—I used to finish) |

| **Parlare** To speak | **Vedere** To see | **Dormire** To sleep |
|---|---|---|
| io parl*avo* | io ved*evo* | io dorm*ivo* |
| tu parl*avi* | tu ved*evi* | tu dorm*ivi* |
| lui parl*ava* | lui ved*eva* | lui dorm*iva* |
| lei parl*ava* | lei ved*eva* | lei dorm*iva* |
| noi parl*avamo* | noi ved*evamo* | noi dorm*ivamo* |
| voi parl*avate* | voi ved*evate* | voi dorm*ivate* |
| loro parl*avano* | loro ved*evano* | loro dorm*ivano* |

## 3. Practice

Write the *imperfect tense* of the verbs.

1. **pensare**     io _____   tu _____   lui, lei _____

   (to think)    noi _____   voi _____   loro _____

2. **bere**     io _____   tu _____   lui, lei _____

   (to drink)    noi _____   voi _____   loro _____

3. **finire**     io _____   tu _____   lui, lei _____

   (to finish)    noi _____   voi _____   loro _____

4. **abitare**     io _____   tu _____   lui, lei _____

   (to live)    noi _____   voi _____   loro _____

# 4. Practice

Write the verbs in the *imperfect tense* in the person indicated.

**Io:**

mangiare                    mettere                    sentire

_____            _____            _____


**Tu:**

cantare                     vedere                     finire

_____            _____            _____


**Lui, Lei:**

saltare                     bere                       aprire

_____            _____            _____


**Noi:**

votare                      rispondere                 costruire

_____            _____            _____


**Voi:**

giocare                     comprendere                applaudire

_____            _____            _____


**Loro:**

sperare                     vendere                    preferire

_____            _____            _____

## 5. Practice

**A.** Write the *imperfect* of the verbs.

1. Lui (parlare) _____

2. Voi (cantare) _____

3. Lui (abitare) _____

4. Noi (partire) _____

5. Voi (giocare) _____

6. Loro (finire) _____

7. Io (camminare) _____

8. Tu (perdere) _____

9. Voi (comprendere) _____

10. Loro (mangiare) _____

11. Tu (costruire) _____

12. Voi (istruire) _____

13. Lui (lavorare) _____

14. Lei (ballare) _____

15. Loro (pensare) _____

16. Voi (credere) _____

17. Tu (lavare) _____

18. Noi (scrivere) _____

19. Io (correre) _____

20. Lei (parlare) _____

**B.** Rewrite in English.

1. Mangiavamo _____

2. Studiavi _____

3. Bevevi _____

4. Giocavi _____

5. Sentiva _____

6. Capivate _____

7. Scrivevano _____

8. Chiedevo _____

9. Chiudevate _____

10. Ascoltava _____

11. Prendevamo _____

12. Imparavo _____

13. Vendevamo _____

14. Vendevi _____

15. Capivi _____

16. Vivevano _____

17. Istruiva _____

18. Vedeva _____

19. Ricevevano _____

20. Insegnavo _____

## 6. Practice

Rewrite in Italian, using the *imperfect.*

1. They used to eat _____
2. We were thinking _____
3. You (s.) were coming _____
4. I believed _____
5. They didn't think _____
6. I was learning _____
7. They believed _____
8. We used to ask _____
9. You (s.) didn't want _____
10. He was waiting _____
11. They were learning _____
12. I understood _____
13. You could _____
14. We used to sing _____
15. They wanted _____
16. I thought _____
17. We thought _____
18. He wanted _____
19. He used to go _____
20. I was waiting _____
21. I was hoping _____
22. We used to hope _____
23. I used to speak _____

24. Were you studying? _____
25. Were you speaking? _____
26. He was hoping _____
27. You (s.) thought _____
28. We were working _____
29. They wanted _____
30. We used to look _____
31. Were we looking? _____
32. He used to travel _____
33. I was teaching _____
34. They used to eat _____
35. I didn't understand _____
36. I couldn't _____
37. They used to sing _____
38. They didn't want _____
39. I didn't think _____
40. You (s.) thought _____
41. She wanted _____
42. I used to clean _____
43. We were looking _____
44. They weren't hoping _____
45. He was hoping _____
46. You (s.) doubted _____

# Passato Remoto (Preterit)

## 7. Uses of the Passato Remoto

The *passato remoto* is a past tense, also called the historical past. It is mostly used in narrative writing of events of the past.

The *passato remoto* and the *passato prossimo* (a compound tense found in the next chapter) are similar since they both express an action in the past. They are commonly translated into English by the simple past, e.g., I bought, we played.

The *passato prossimo* is commonly used in speaking about the past. On the other hand, the *passato remoto* is mostly used in writing but is sometimes used in speaking, when the action is considered distant and not connected to the present.

## 8. Forms of the Passato Remoto

The *passato remoto* is formed by putting the correct endings to the infinitive roots. Following are the endings of the *passato remoto* for the three conjugations. Many common verbs have irregular roots for the *passato remoto*.

| **Comprare** To buy | **Vendere** To sell | **Sentire** To hear |
|---|---|---|
| io    compr*ai* | vend*ei* | sent*ii* |
| tu    compr*asti* | vend*esti* | sent*isti* |
| lui   compr*ò* | vend*è* | sent*ì* |
| lei   compr*ò* | vend*è* | sent*ì* |
| noi  compr*ammo* | vend*emmo* | sent*immo* |
| voi  compr*aste* | vend*este* | sent*iste* |
| loro compr*arono* | vend*erono* | sent*irono* |

## 9. Practice

Write the *passato remoto* of the verbs.

1. **mangiare**      io _____    tu _____    lui, lei _____
   (to eat)           noi _____   voi _____   loro _____

2. **potere**        io _____    tu _____    lui, lei _____
   (to be able)     noi _____   voi _____   loro _____

3. **capire**        io _____    tu _____    lui, lei _____
   (to understand)   noi _____   voi _____   loro _____

# 10. Common Verbs with Irregular Roots in the Passato Remoto

Many common verbs have irregular roots in the *passato remoto* and they must be learned. The endings are the same as previously shown. Following are some of the most common verbs with irregular roots for the *passato remoto*.

**Accendere:** *Accesi, accendesti, accese, accendemmo, accendeste, accesero*

**Bere:** *Bevvi, bevesti, bevve, bevemmo, beveste, bevvero*

**Cadere:** *Caddi, cadesti, cadde, cademmo, cadeste, caddero*

**Chiedere:** *Chiesi, chiedesti, chiese, chiedemmo, chiedeste, chiesero*

**Chiudere:** *Chiusi, chiudesti, chiuse, chiudemmo, chiudeste, chiusero*

**Cogliere:** *Colsi, cogliesti, colse, cogliemmo, coglieste, colsero*

**Conoscere:** *Conobbi, conoscesti, conobbe, conoscemmo, conosceste, conobbero*

**Dare:** *Diedi, desti, diede, demmo, deste, diedero*

**Decidere:** *Decisi, decidesti, decise, decidemmo, decideste, decisero*

**Dire:** *Dissi, dicesti, disse, dicemmo, diceste, dissero*

**Discutere:** *Discussi, discutesti, discusse, discutemmo, discuteste, discussero*

**Dovere:** *Dovetti, dovesti, dovette, dovemmo, doveste, dovettero*

**Fare:** *Feci, facesti, fece, facemmo, faceste, fecero*

**Leggere:** *Lessi, leggesti, lesse, leggemmo, leggeste, lessero*

**Mettere:** *Misi, mettesti, mise, mettemmo, metteste, misero*

**Nascere:** *Nacqui, nascesti, nacque, nascemmo, nasceste, nacquero*

**Prendere:** *Presi, prendesti, prese, prendemmo, prendeste, presero*

**Porre:** *Posi, ponesti, pose, ponemmo, poneste, posero*

**Ridere:** *Risi, ridesti, rise, ridemmo, rideste, risero*

**Rimanere:** *Rimasi, rimanesti, rimase, rimanemmo, rimaneste, rimasero*

**Sapere:** *Seppi, sapesti, seppe, sapemmo, sapeste, seppero*

**Scegliere:** *Scelsi, scegliesti, scelse, scegliemmo, sceglieste, scelsero*

**Scendere:** *Scesi, scendesti, scese, scendemmo, scendeste, scesero*

**Scrivere:** *Scrissi, scrivesti, scrisse, scrivemmo, scriveste, scrissero*

**Spegnere:** *Spensi, spegnesti, spense, spegnemmo, spegneste, spensero*

**Stare:** *Stetti, stesti, stette, stemmo, steste, stettero*

**Tenere:** *Tenni, tenesti, tenne, tenemmo, teneste, tennero*

**Vedere:** *Vidi, vedesti, vide, vedemmo, vedeste, videro*

**Venire:** *Venni, venisti, venne, venimmo, veniste, vennero*

**Vincere:** *Vinsi, vincesti, vinse, vincemmo, vinceste, vinsero*

**Vivere:** *Vissi, vivesti, visse, vivemmo, viveste, vissero*

**Volere:** *Volli, volesti, volle, volemmo, voleste, vollero*

## 11. Practice

Write the *passato remoto* of the verbs in the person indicated.

**Io:**

chiedere

_____

conoscere

_____

sentire

_____

**Tu:**

comprare

_____

temere

_____

finire

_____

**Carlo:**

nascere

_____

vedere

_____

volere

_____

**Maria:**

capire

_____

scrivere

_____

venire

_____

**Noi:**

fare

_____

bere

_____

ridere

_____

**Voi:**

scendere

_____

vincere

_____

mettere

_____

**Loro:**

offrire

_____

partire

_____

fare

_____

## 12. Practice

Rewrite in English.

1. Io venni _____
2. Io risi _____
3. Io bevvi _____
4. Lui cadde _____
5. Lei chiese _____
6. Noi chiudemmo _____
7. Voi conosceste _____
8. Tu dicesti _____
9. Lei decise _____
10. Noi dicemmo _____
11. Voi doveste _____
12. Loro dissero _____
13. Io vissi _____
14. Loro vinsero _____
15. Tu facesti _____
16. Lei lesse _____
17. Noi leggemmo _____
18. Tu mettesti _____
19. Voi nasceste _____
20. Io presi _____

21. Noi prendemmo _____
22. Tu ridesti _____
23. Loro risero _____
24. Lei rimase _____
25. Tu scegliesti _____
26. Loro scrissero _____
27. Io scelsi _____
28. Tu scegliesti _____
29. Loro scrissero _____
30. Voi steste _____
31. Tu vedesti _____
32. Noi vedemmo _____
33. Voi vinceste _____
34. Io vidi _____
35. Loro videro _____
36. Lei visse _____
37. Lui volle _____
38. Noi volemmo _____
39. Loro vennero _____
40. Tu stesti _____

# 13. Review Practice

Practices 13 and 14 review the *present, imperative, imperfect, future,* and *passato remoto.*
Rewrite in English.

1. Parlo _____

2. Mangiamo _____

3. Abitano _____

4. Abitate? _____

5. Guidiamo _____

6. Non lavoro _____

7. Ritorneremo _____

8. Ritorneranno _____

9. Non volo _____

10. Volate? _____

11. Arriveranno _____

12. Arriverò _____

13. Non arriverete _____

14. Chiedo _____

15. Non chiedevo _____

16. Chiudono _____

17. Chiudi? _____

18. Penso _____

19. Penserai _____

20. Riposiamo _____

21. Riposano _____

22. Non riposi _____

23. Parlai _____

24. Pensammo _____

25. Riposi? _____

26. Mangia! _____

27. Guardate! _____

28. Parlate! _____

29. Impara! _____

30. Non guardare! _____

31. Non dormire! _____

32. Senta! _____

33. Prometti? _____

34. Risponderò _____

35. Scriveremo _____

36. Leggevo _____

37. Parlavi _____

38. Volevate _____

39. Piangevano _____

40. Insistevi _____

41. Bevevi _____

42. Bevi! _____

43. Bevete! _____

44. Non bere! _____

45. Vieni _____

46. Vieni? _____

47. Lesse _____

48. Sentiste _____

## 14. Review Practice

Rewrite in Italian.

1. They live _____
2. I used to open _____
3. They worked _____
4. We climb _____
5. I understand _____
6. They ate _____
7. We ate _____
8. He works _____
9. They study _____
10. I keep _____
11. I write _____
12. You (s.) used to write _____
13. I'll write _____
14. You (s.) travel _____
15. You (s.) used to travel _____
16. They'll travel _____
17. I leave _____
18. He leaves _____
19. We'll leave _____
20. She was leaving _____
21. He was learning _____
22. We were learning _____
23. They thought _____

24. I'll live _____
25. We'll open _____
26. Eat (s.)! _____
27. Work (s.)! _____
28. He'll eat _____
29. He'll work _____
30. Study (s.)! _____
31. Study (pl.)! _____
32. Drink (s.)! _____
33. Drink (pl.)! _____
34. We promised _____
35. I wanted _____
36. She must _____
37. Answer (s.)! _____
38. Write (s.) (formal)! _____
39. Speak (s.) (formal)! _____
40. I said _____
41. We'll wait _____
42. I discuss _____
43. We used to see _____
44. They know _____
45. We understand _____
46. I used to think _____

# Chapter 5

## *Essere* (to Be) and *Avere* (to Have)

### 1. Forms of *Essere* and *Avere*

It is important to become familiar with the irregular verbs **essere** and **avere**, two of the most commonly used verbs in Italian. Besides being used alone in the usual conjugations, they are also used to form the compound tenses.

Following are the complete conjugations of **essere** and **avere.** (Note that some of the tenses will be covered in later chapters.)

*Essere*

**Present Indicative**
*sono, sei, è, siamo, siete, sono*

**Imperfect**
*ero, eri, era, eravamo,*
*eravate, erano*

**Future**
*sarò, sarai, sarà, saremo,*
*sarete, saranno*

**Imperative**
*sii, siamo, siate*
*sia (pol. s.), siano (pol. pl.)*

**Passato Remoto (Preterit)**
*fui, fosti, fu, fummo*
*foste, furono*

**Passato Prossimo (Present Perfect)**
*sono stato/a, sei stato/a, è stato/a,*
*siamo stati/e, siete stati/e, sono stati/e*

**Trapassato Prossimo (Pluperfect)**
*ero stato/a, eri stato/a, era stato/a,*
*eravamo stati/e, eravate stati/e,*
*erano stati/e*

*Avere*

**Present Indicative**
*ho, hai, ha, abbiamo, avete, hanno*

**Imperfect**
*avevo, avevi, aveva, avevamo,*
*avevate, avevano*

**Future**
*avrò, avrai, avrà, avremo,*
*avrete, avranno*

**Imperative**
*abbi, abbiamo, abbiate*
*abbia (pol. s.), abbiano (pol. pl.)*

**Passato Remoto (Preterit)**
*ebbi, avesti, ebbe, avemmo,*
*aveste, ebbero*

**Passato Prossimo (Present Perfect)**
*ho avuto, hai avuto, ha avuto,*
*abbiamo avuto, avete avuto,*
*hanno avuto*

**Trapassato Prossimo (Pluperfect)**
*avevo avuto, avevi avuto, aveva*
*avuto, avevamo avuto, avevate*
*avuto, avevano avuto*

| *Essere* | *Avere* |
|---|---|
| **Present Conditional** | |
| *sarei, saresti, sarebbe, saremmo, sareste, sarebbero* | *avrei, avresti, avrebbe, avremmo, avreste, avrebbero* |
| **Past Conditional** | |
| *sarei stato/a, saresti stato/a, sarebbe stato/a, saremmo stati/e, sareste stati/e, sarebbero stati/e* | *avrei avuto, avresti avuto, avrebbe, avuto, avremmo avuto, avreste avuto, avrebbero avuto* |
| **Present Subjunctive** | |
| *che io sia, tu sia, lui/lei sia, noi siamo, voi siate, loro siano* | *che io abbia, tu abbia, lui/lei abbia, noi abbiamo, voi abbiate, loro abbiano* |
| **Imperfect Subjunctive** | |
| *che io fossi, tu fossi, lui/lei fosse, noi fossimo, voi foste, loro fossero* | *che io avessi, tu avessi, lui/lei avesse, noi avessimo, voi aveste, loro avessero* |
| **Past Subjunctive** | |
| *che io sia stato/a, tu sia stato/a, lui/lei sia stato/a, noi siano stati/e, voi siate stati/e, loro siano stati/e* | *che io abbia avuto, tu abbia avuto, lui/lei abbia avuto, noi abbiamo avuto, voi abbiate avuto, loro abbiano avuto* |
| **Pluperfect Subjunctive** | |
| *che io fossi stato/a, tu fossi stato/a, lui/lei fosse stato/a, noi fossimo stati/e, voi foste stati/e, loro fossero stati/e* | *che io avessi avuto, tu avessi avuto, lui/lei avesse avuto, noi avessimo avuto, voi aveste avuto, loro avessero avuto* |

*Essere*

*Avere*

# Passato Prossimo with *Avere*

## 2. Uses of the Passato Prossimo

The *passato prossimo* (present perfect) is used to describe actions and events that occurred in the recent past. It is often preceded or followed by such time expressions as *ieri, domenica scorsa, l'anno scorso, un anno fa, un'ora fa.*

## 3. Forms of the Passato Prossimo with *Avere*

The *passato prossimo* of most Italian verbs is formed by the present tense of the auxiliary verb *avere* and the past participle of the verb.

| | | | |
|---|---|---|---|
| **Examples:** | *io* | *ho mangiato* | I have eaten |
| | *tu* | *hai mangiato* | you have eaten |
| | *lui* | *ha mangiato* | he has caten |
| | *lei* | *ha mangiato* | she has eaten |
| | *noi* | *abbiamo mangiato* | we have eaten |
| | *voi* | *avete mangiato* | you have eaten |
| | *loro* | *hanno mangiato* | they have eaten |

The *past participle* is formed, for regular verbs, by adding:

*ato* to the infinitive root of *-are* verbs
*uto* to the infinitive root of *-ere* verbs
*ito* to the infinitive root of *-ire* verbs

| | | | |
|---|---|---|---|
| **Infinitive:** | *parlare* (to speak) | *vedere* (to see) | *sentire* (to hear) |
| **Past Participle:** | *parlato* (spoken) | *veduto* (seen) | *sentito* (heard) |

In English, the *passato prossimo* is translated either with the simple past or the present perfect.

| | | |
|---|---|---|
| **Examples:** | *Ho mangiato* alle otto. | I *ate* at eight o'clock. |
| | *Ho mangiato* tardi. | I *have* eaten late. |

**Note:** With the verb *avere,* the past participle doesn't agree in gender and number with the subject. The negative is formed by placing *non* in front of *avere.* If there is a second negative, this follows *avere.*

| | | |
|---|---|---|
| **Examples:** | *Non ho parlato* molto. | I didn't talk a lot. |
| | *Non ho mai parlato* molto. | I never talked a lot. |

# Passato Prossimo with *Essere*

## 4. Forms of the Passato Prossimo with *Essere*

The *passato prossimo* of several Italian verbs is formed with the auxiliary verb *essere* plus the past participle. The past participle agrees in gender and in number with the subject.

| Examples: | Masculine | | Feminine | |
|---|---|---|---|---|
| | io | sono andato | io | sono andata |
| | tu | sei andato | tu | sei andata |
| | lui | è andato | lei | è andata |
| | noi | siamo andati | noi | siamo andate |
| | voi | siete andati | voi | siete andate |
| | loro | sono andati | loro | sono andate |

## 5. Common Verbs with *Essere* in the Passato Prossimo

Following is a list of commonly used verbs that form the *passato prossimo* with *essere*.

| | | | |
|---|---|---|---|
| **accadere** | to happen | *E' accaduto un incidente.* | An accident happened. |
| **andare** | to go | *Sono andato/a a scuola.* | I went to school. |
| **arrivare** | to arrive | *È arrivata tardi.* | She arrived late. |
| **diventare** | to become | *È diventato famoso.* | He became famous. |
| **entrare** | to enter | *Sono entrato/a.* | I went inside. |
| **morire** | to die | *Il cane è morto.* | The dog died. |
| **nascere** | to be born | *Sono nati/e ieri.* | They were born yesterday. |
| **partire** | to depart | *Gianni è già partito.* | John left already. |
| **restare** | to remain | *Lei è restata a casa.* | She remained at home. |
| **rimanere** | to remain | *Lui è rimasto a casa.* | He remained at home. |
| **scendere** | to descend | *Siamo scesi/e in fretta.* | We descended in a hurry. |
| **stare** | to stay | *Sono state a casa.* | They stayed home. |
| **tornare** | to return | *Siete tornati tardi.* | You returned late. |
| **uscire** | to go out | *È appena uscito.* | He just went out. |
| **venire** | to come | *Sono venuto/a in America.* | I came to America. |

# Irregular Past Participles

## 6. List of Irregular Past Participles

Many Italian verbs, especially *-ere* verbs, have irregular past participles.

Following is a list of the most common verbs with irregular *past participles:*

| Infinitive | | Past Participle |
|---|---|---|
| **accendere** | to turn on | *acceso* |
| **aggiungere** | to add | *aggiunto* |
| **apparire** | to appear | *apparso* |
| **appendere** | to hang | *appeso* |
| **apprendere** | to learn | *appreso* |
| **aprire** | to open | *aperto* |
| **assumere** | to hire | *assunto* |
| **bere** | to drink | *bevuto* |
| **chiedere** | to ask | *chiesto* |
| **chiudere** | to close | *chiuso* |
| **cogliere** | to gather | *colto* |
| **comprendere** | to comprehend | *compreso* |
| **concludere** | to conclude | *concluso* |
| **confondere** | to confuse | *confuso* |
| **conoscere** | to know | *conosciuto* |
| **convincere** | to convince | *convinto* |
| **coprire** | to cover | *coperto* |
| **correre** | to run | *corso* |
| **correggere** | to correct | *corretto* |
| **cuocere** | to cook | *cotto* |
| **decidere** | to decide | *deciso* |
| **difendere** | to defend | *difeso* |
| **dire** | to tell, say | *detto* |
| **discutere** | to discuss | *discusso* |
| **distinguere** | to distinguish | *distinto* |
| **dividere** | to divide | *diviso* |
| **eleggere** | to elect | *eletto* |
| **esprimere** | to express | *espresso* |
| **fare** | to make, do | *fatto* |
| **includere** | to include | *incluso* |
| **interrompere** | to interrupt | *interrotto* |
| **leggere** | to read | *letto* |

| Infinitive | | Past Participle |
|---|---|---|
| mettere | to put | *messo* |
| morire | to die | *morto* |
| muovere | to move | *mosso* |
| nascere | to be born | *nato* |
| nascondere | to hide | *nascosto* |
| offrire | to offer | *offerto* |
| perdere | to lose | *perso* |
| permettere | to permit | *permesso* |
| prendere | to take, get | *preso* |
| promettere | to promise | *promesso* |
| promuovere | to promote | *promosso* |
| proporre | to propose | *proposto* |
| porre | to put | *posto* |
| proteggere | to protect | *protetto* |
| provvedere | to provide | *provvisto* |
| raggiungere | to reach | *raggiunto* |
| richiedere | to request | *richiesto* |
| ridere | to laugh | *riso* |
| ridurre | to reduce | *ridotto* |
| rimanere | to remain | *rimasto* |
| rimuovere | to remove | *rimosso* |
| risolvere | to resolve | *risolto* |
| rispondere | to answer | *risposto* |
| rompere | to break | *rotto* |
| scegliere | to choose | *scelto* |
| scendere | to descend | *sceso* |
| scomparire | to disappear | *scomparso* |
| scrivere | to write | *scritto* |
| soffrire | to suffer | *sofferto* |
| sorridere | to smile | *sorriso* |
| spegnere | to turn off | *spento* |
| spendere | to spend | *speso* |
| spingere | to push | *spinto* |
| succedere | to happen | *successo* |
| togliere | to remove | *tolto* |
| trasmettere | to broadcast | *trasmesso* |
| vedere | to see | *visto* |
| vincere | to win | *vinto* |
| vivere | to live | *vissuto* |

# 7. Practice

Write the *passato prossimo* of the verbs.

1. **mangiare**     io _____     tu _____     lui, lei _____
   (to eat)         noi _____     voi _____     loro _____

2. **scrivere**     io _____     tu _____     lui, lei _____
   (to write)       noi _____     voi _____     loro _____

3. **venire**       io _____     tu _____     lui, lei _____
   (to come)        noi _____     voi _____     loro _____

4. **andare**       io _____     tu _____     lui, lei _____
   (to go)          noi _____     voi _____     loro _____

# 8. Practice

Write the verb in the *passato prossimo* in the person indicated.

**Io:**

| mangiare | vedere | sentire |
|---|---|---|
| | | |

**Tu:**

| parlare | scrivere | capire |
|---|---|---|
| | | |

**Lui:**

| viaggiare | potere | finire |
|---|---|---|
| | | |

**Lei:**

| camminare | volere | venire |
|---|---|---|
| | | |

**Noi:**

| lodare | spingere | salire |
|---|---|---|
| | | |

**Voi:**

| stare | ridere | aprire |
|---|---|---|
| | | |

**Loro:**

| dare | rimanere | nutrire |
|---|---|---|
| | | |

**Carlo:**

| fare | nascere | offrire |
|---|---|---|
| | | |

**Maria:**

| andare | nascondere | pulire |
|---|---|---|
| | | |

**Io e Giovanni:**

| aspettare | vendere | partire |
|---|---|---|
| | | |

**Tu e Pietro:**

| imparare | chiudere | uscire |
|---|---|---|
| | | |

**Giovanni e Paolo:**

| fermare | vivere | finire |
|---|---|---|
| | | |

# 9. Practice

Write the verbs in the *passato prossimo*, using the negative in the person indicated.

**Io:**

essere                      avere                       potere

_____             _____             _____


**Tu:**

volere                      dovere                      capire

_____             _____             _____


**Lui:**

fare                        dare                        stare

_____             _____             _____


**Noi:**

andare                      arrivare                    partire

_____             _____             _____

## 10. Practice

Write the verbs in the *passato prossimo* in the person indicated by the subject.

1. Lui (parlare) _____
2. Noi (stare) _____
3. Lei (stare) _____
4. Voi (leggere) _____
5. Loro (sentire) _____
6. Io (dormire) _____
7. Tu (perdere) _____
8. Lei (andare) _____
9. Lui (decidere) _____
10. Noi (comprare) _____
11. Voi (vivere) _____
12. Loro (bere) _____
13. Lui (parlare) _____
14. Lei (aprire) _____
15. Lui (aprire) _____
16. Voi (imparare) _____
17. Noi (temere) _____

18. Io (mangiare) _____
19. Tu (ricevere) _____
20. Lui (lavorare) _____
21. Noi (viaggiare) _____
22. Loro (potere) _____
23. Voi (insegnare) _____
24. Noi (sciare) _____
25. Noi (correre) _____
26. Io (guardare) _____
27. Tu (guarire) _____
28. Voi (rispondere) _____
29. Loro (arrivare) _____
30. Noi (tenere) _____
31. Lei (vendere) _____
32. Loro (vivere) _____
33. Io (abitare) _____
34. Noi (gettare) _____

## 11. Practice

Write the verbs in the *passato prossimo,* using the negative in the person indicated.

1. Lui (mangiare) _____
2. Lei (comprare) _____
3. Tu (parlare) _____
4. Io (studiare) _____
5. Loro (dovere) _____

6. Noi (cantare) _____
7. Loro (vedere) _____
8. Voi (sentire) _____
9. Tu (scrivere) _____
10. Noi (volere) _____

## 12. Practice

Rewrite in Italian, using the *passato prossimo.*

1. We answered _____
2. They bought _____
3. We learned _____
4. She bought _____
5. I asked _____
6. You (s.) answered _____
7. We left _____
8. I drank _____
9. I didn't drink _____
10. They taught _____
11. I read_____
12. You (s.) wrote _____
13. They worked _____
14. He slept _____
15. She worked _____
16. We studied _____
17. He didn't ski _____
18. She didn't go _____
19. She was born _____

20. They sold _____
21. I didn't listen _____
22. I didn't hear _____
23. I didn't ask_____
24. You (s.) didn't answer_____
25. I received _____
26. I learned _____
27. They understood_____
28. She traveled _____
29. We didn't travel _____
30. They cleaned _____
31. We thought _____
32. They didn't think _____
33. I cleaned_____
34. You (s.) paid _____
35. You (s.) didn't pay_____
36. We ate_____
37. I arrived _____
38. They stayed _____

# Trapassato Prossimo

## 13. Forms of the Trapassato Prossimo

The *trapassato prossimo* (pluperfect) is formed by using the imperfect of the auxiliary verbs *avere* or *essere*, plus the *past participle.*

| **Examples:** | | | | |
|---|---|---|---|---|
| | *avevo mangiato* | I had eaten | *ero andato/a* | I had gone |
| | *avevi mangiato* | you had eaten | *eri andato/a* | you had gone |
| | *aveva mangiato* | he had eaten | *era andato* | he had gone |
| | *aveva mangiato* | she had eaten | *era andata* | she had gone |
| | *avevamo mangiato* | we had eaten | *eravamo andati/e* | we had gone |
| | *avevate mangiato* | you had eaten | *eravate andati/e* | you had gone |
| | *avevano mangiato* | they had eaten | *erano andati/e* | they had gone |

## 14. Uses of the Trapassato Prossimo

This tense is used to express an action in the past that had happened before another one. The more recent past action can be expressed in the *passato prossimo, passato remoto,* or *imperfect.*

| **Examples:** | Dove è stato Giulio? | Where did Giulio go? |
|---|---|---|
| | È andato in vacanza | He went on vacation |
| | dove *era stato* tanti | where he had been |
| | anni fa. | many years ago. |

## 15. Practice

Write the *trapassato prossimo* of the verbs.

1. **guardare**    io _____    tu _____    lui, lei _____
   (to look)    noi _____    voi _____    loro _____

2. **vedere**    io _____    tu _____    lui, lei _____
   (to see)    noi _____    voi _____    loro _____

3. **partire**    io _____    tu _____    lui, lei _____
   (to leave)    noi _____    voi _____    loro _____

# 16. Practice

Write the verbs in the *trapassato prossimo* in the person indicated.

**Io:**

mangiare                     vedere                     sentire

_____              _____            _____

**Tu:**

parlare                      credere                    pulire

_____              _____            _____

**Lui, Lei:**

visitare                     scrivere                   finire

_____              _____            _____

**Noi:**

arrivare                     bere                       capire

_____              _____            _____

**Voi:**

comprare                     leggere                    venire

_____              _____            _____

**Loro:**

dare                         potere                     aprire

_____              _____            _____

**Carlo:**

giocare                      spingere                   costruire

_____              _____            _____

**Carlo e Maria:**

viaggiare                    vendere                    partire

_____              _____            _____

## 17. Practice

Rewrite in Italian, using the *trapassato prossimo*.

1. I had understood _____

2. You had gone _____

3. She had studied _____

4. He had drunk _____

5. We had finished _____

6. You (pl.) had slept _____

7. They had bought _____

8. I had worked _____

9. You (s.) had thought _____

10. He had played _____

11. We had traveled _____

12. You (pl.) had cleaned _____

13. They had watched _____

14. I had been _____

15. You (s.) had arrived _____

16. He had left _____

17. She had gone _____

18. We had read _____

19. You (pl.) had written _____

20. They had finished _____

21. I had won _____

22. He had lost _____

23. She had gone _____

24. We had listened _____

## 18. Review Practice

This practice reviews the *passato prossimo* and *trapassato prossimo*.
Rewrite in Italian.

1.  I have eaten _____

2.  You (s.) had eaten _____

3.  She has gone _____

4.  He had come _____

5.  We have finished _____

6.  We had finished _____

7.  You (pl.) have seen _____

8.  You (pl.) had looked _____

9.  They have read _____

10. They had read _____

11. I have played _____

12. I had slept _____

13. He has eaten _____

14. We had skied _____

15. We have not read _____

16. We had not thought _____

17. They have not won _____

18. They had not promised _____

19. I have not chosen _____

20. He has not come _____

21. She had not left _____

22. We have lived _____

23. We have not lived _____

24. We had lived _____

# Chapter 6

## Conditional

### 1. Uses of the Conditional

The conditional *(condizionale)* is used to refer to an action or state that *may* happen if something else occurred or if some condition were present. In English, the conditional is indicated by *would.*

> **Example:** Al tuo posto *studierei* di più.     In your place I would study more.

The conditional is used to add politeness or kindness to wishes and demands.

> **Examples:** *Vorrei* un caffè.     I would like a coffee.
> Mi *faresti* un favore?     Would you do me a favor?

### 2. Forms of the Conditional

The *present conditional* tense is made up of the future root plus the conditional endings, which are the same for all three conjugations.

| **Cantare** (To sing) | **Vendere** (To sell) | **Sentire** (To hear) |
|---|---|---|
| io      canter*ei* | vender*ei* | sentir*ei* |
| tu      canter*esti* | vender*esti* | sentir*esti* |
| lui     canter*ebbe* | vender*ebbe* | sentir*ebbe* |
| lei     canter*ebbe* | vender*ebbe* | sentir*ebbe* |
| noi     canter*emmo* | vender*emmo* | sentir*emmo* |
| voi     canter*este* | vender*este* | sentir*este* |
| loro    canter*ebbero* | vender*ebbero* | sentir*ebbero* |

**Note:** Remember the use of *e* in the stem for *-are* verbs.

Verbs ending in *-care* and *-gare* add an *h* in the conditional to keep the hard *c* and *g* sounds: *pagherei, giocherei.*

Verbs ending in *-ciare* and *-giare* drop the *i* in the conditional: *comincerei, mangerei.*

Verbs that have irregular roots in the future use the same irregular roots in the conditional. Following are the most common verbs that have irregular roots:

| andare | **andr** | *andrei, andresti, etc.* |
|--------|----------|--------------------------|
| bere   | **berr** | *berrei, berresti, etc.* |
| cadere | **cadr** | *cadrei, cadresti, etc.* |
| dare   | **dar**  | *darei, daresti, etc.*   |
| dovere | **dovr** | *dovrei, dovresti, etc.* |
| essere | **sar**  | *sarei, saresti, etc.*   |
| fare   | **far**  | *farei, faresti, etc.*   |
| potere | **potr** | *potrei, potresti, etc.* |
| sapere | **sapr** | *saprei, sapresti, etc.* |
| valere | **varr** | *varrei, varresti, etc.* |
| vedere | **vedr** | *vedrei, vedresti, etc.* |
| venire | **verr** | *verrei, verresti, etc.* |
| volere | **vorr** | *vorrei, vorresti, etc.* |

**Note:** The conditional of *dovere* is translated as *should.*

# 3. Practice

Write the *present conditional* of the verbs.

1. **andare**       io _____ tu _____ lui, lei _____
   (to go)        noi _____ voi _____ loro _____

2. **dovere**       io _____ tu _____ lui, lei _____
   (to have to, must)   noi _____ voi _____ loro _____

3. **venire**       io _____ tu _____ lui, lei _____
   (to come)      noi _____ voi _____ loro _____

# 4. Practice

Write the verbs in the *present conditional* in the person indicated.

**Io:**
cantare                    potere                    capire

_____    _____    _____

**Tu:**
ballare                    vedere                    dormire

_____    _____    _____

**Lui, Lei:**
nuotare                    bere                    sentire

_____    _____    _____

**Noi:**
ordinare                    leggere                    finire

_____    _____    _____

**Voi:**
viaggiare                    dovere                    partire

_____    _____    _____

**Loro:**
domandare                    volere                    venire

_____    _____    _____

**Giovanna:**
ascoltare                    avere                    dire

_____    _____    _____

**Io e Carlo:**
parlare                    vedere                    colpire

_____    _____    _____

**Tu e Giovanna:**
desiderare                    vincere                    ubbidire

_____    _____    _____

**Giovanna e Carlo:**
organizzare                    promettere                    offrire

_____    _____    _____

# 5. Practice

Write the verbs in the *negative* of the *present conditional.*

**Io:**

parlare                    vedere                    sentire

_____            _____           _____


**Tu:**

viaggiare                  scrivere                  pulire

_____            _____           _____


**Paolo:**

mangiare                   potere                    capire

_____            _____           _____


**Io e Carlo:**

studiare                   leggere                   finire

_____            _____           _____


**Tu e Paolo:**

arrivare                   volere                    partire

_____            _____           _____

# 6. Practice

Rewrite in English.

1. Comprerei _____

2. Vedresti _____

3. Capirei _____

4. Non mangeremmo _____

5. Verreste _____

6. Sentirebbero _____

7. Studierei _____

8. Non studierei _____

9. Viaggeresti _____

10. Capirebbe _____

11. Carla arriverebbe _____

12. Saremmo _____

13. Scriverebbero _____

14. Dormirei _____

15. Non leggeresti _____

16. Paolo non partirebbe _____

17. Faremmo _____

18. Non giochereste _____

19. Sareste _____

20. Ascolterebbero _____

21. Verrei _____

22. Non verrei _____

23. Staresti _____

24. Carlo capirebbe _____

25. Maria cucinerebbe _____

26. Giocheremmo _____

27. Vorremmo _____

28. Non vorremmo _____

29. Tu e Paolo fareste _____

30. Non farei _____

31. Andremmo _____

32. Portereste _____

33. Carla non porterebbe _____

34. Dovrebbero _____

35. Inviterei _____

36. Verrebbero _____

## Interrogative Forms

1. Verresti? _____

2. Canterebbero? _____

3. Capirebbe? _____

4. Dareste? _____

5. Parlerebbe? _____

6. Sentiresti? _____

7. Faremmo? _____

8. Cucineresti? _____

# 7. Practice

Rewrite in Italian, using the *present conditional.*

1. I would think _____
2. I would drink _____
3. You could _____
4. He would do _____
5. He would not do _____
6. She would write _____
7. I would work _____
8. They would drink _____
9. I would clean _____
10. She would make _____
11. They would wash _____
12. I would watch _____
13. They would see _____
14. We would think _____
15. I would wash _____
16. You (s.) would understand _____
17. They would not go _____
18. You (pl.) would see _____
19. I would not take _____
20. I would know _____

21. You (s.) would go _____
22. You (s.) could not _____
23. She would think _____
24. We would write _____
25. They would read _____
26. I would sleep _____
27. They could not _____
28. We would eat _____
29. I would drink _____
30. You (pl.) would travel _____
31. She would return _____
32. He would arrive _____
33. They would leave _____
34. I would not arrive _____
35. She would not plant _____
36. He would win _____
37. They would eat _____
38. We would swim _____
39. You (pl.) would ski _____
40. We would look _____

# 8. Practice

Rewrite in Italian. Use the conditional of *dovere.*

1. I should go _____
2. You (s.) should write _____
3. They should study _____
4. We should come _____
5. He should cook _____
6. She should read _____

# Past Conditional

## 9. Forms of the Past Conditional

The *past conditional (condizionale passato)* is a compound tense. It is formed by the conditional tense of the auxiliary *avere* or *essere* plus the past participle of the main verb. The past participle agrees with the subject when the verb is conjugated with the auxiliary *essere*.

## 10. Uses of the Past Conditional

The *past conditional* is used in dependent clauses to express an action that is considered future as viewed from the past. In English the present conditional is used, but in Italian the past conditional is used.

| | | |
|---|---|---|
| **Example:** | Ha detto che *avrebbe scritto.* | He said that he would write (he would have written). |

The *condizionale passato* of *dovere* followed by an infinitive expresses an obligation that was not done.

| | | |
|---|---|---|
| **Example:** | *Avresti dovuto scrivere* a tua mamma. | You should have written to your mother. |

The *condizionale passato* is also used in sentences with *se* clauses. These will be studied in the next chapter.

## 11. Practice

Write the *past conditional* of the verbs.

1. **parlare**    io _____    tu _____    lui, lei _____
   (to speak)    noi _____    voi _____    loro _____

2. **vedere**    io _____    tu _____    lui, lei _____
   (to see)    noi _____    voi _____    loro _____

3. **venire**    io _____    tu _____    lui, lei _____
   (to come)    noi _____    voi _____    loro _____

# 12. Practice

Write the verbs in the *past conditional* in the person indicated.

**Io:**

andare           ritornare           partire

_____      _____      _____

**Tu:**

parlare           vedere           capire

_____      _____      _____

**Lui, Lei:**

arrivare           scrivere           dormire

_____      _____      _____

**Noi:**

informare           leggere           preferire

_____      _____      _____

**Voi:**

aspettare           dovere           finire

_____      _____      _____

**Loro:**

abitare           bere           uscire

_____      _____      _____

**Carlo:**

invitare           volere           sentire

_____      _____      _____

## 13. Review Practice

Practices 13 and 14 review the *present conditional* and the *past conditional*.
Rewrite in English.

1. Io avrei aspettato _____

2. Tu parleresti _____

3. Avrebbe mangiato _____

4. Capirebbero _____

5. Scrivereste _____

6. Avreste scritto _____

7. Risponderebbero _____

8. Non avrebbe risposto _____

9. Sentirei _____

10. Avrei sentito _____

11. Avremmo firmato _____

12. Inviterei _____

13. Uscireste _____

14. Finiremmo _____

15. Avrebbero finito _____

16. Comprereste _____

17. (Lui) comprerebbe _____

18. Troveresti _____

19. Avrei guardato _____

20. Risponderebbe _____

21. Avrebbe risposto _____

22. Avreste scritto _____

23. Saprei _____

24. Avrebbe saputo _____

## 14. Review Practice

Rewrite in Italian.

1. I would go _____

2. You (s.) would have taken _____

3. We would have danced _____

4. They would have come _____

5. She would know _____

6. We would wait _____

7. We would have started _____

8. She would write _____

9. He would have answered _____

10. They would speak _____

11. They should have come _____

12. I should have spoken _____

13. She should wait _____

14. She should have waited _____

15. We would understand _____

16. They would have understood _____

17. She would have written _____

18. You (s.) would have answered _____

19. You (s.) should have answered _____

20. They would travel _____

21. I would have returned _____

22. He would have left _____

23. She would arrive _____

24. We would leave _____

# Chapter 7

# Present Subjunctive

## 1. Uses of the Subjunctive

The subjunctive *(congiuntivo)* is used very frequently in Italian, while in English it is used very rarely. In Italian, the subjunctive is generally used in a dependent *che* clause and reflects the wishes, hopes, emotions, opinions, feelings, and doubts of the subject.

It is used mainly after the following verbs: *pensare, credere, sperare, dubitare, non sapere, avere paura, volere.* The verb in the main clause is in the indicative, and the *che* clause is in the subjunctive.

| Examples: | Spero *che tu venga.* | I hope that you come. |
|---|---|---|
| | Vogliono *che io venga.* | They want me to come. |

If there is no change of subject, the infinitive is used instead of the subjunctive after the verbs. The preposition *di* is used with certain verbs such as *sperare, avere voglia, avere paura.*

| Examples: | *Ho voglia di andare.* | I have a desire to go. |
|---|---|---|
| | *Spero di vederlo.* | I hope to see him/it. |

## 2. Forms of the Present Subjunctive

The *present subjunctive* is formed by putting the endings of the subjunctive on the infinitive root. Following are the conjugations of the present subjunctive of regular *-are, -ere, -ire* verbs.

| Che + pronoun | Parlare | Vedere | Sentire |
|---|---|---|---|
| che io | parl*i* | ved*a* | sent*a* |
| che tu | parl*i* | ved*a* | sent*a* |
| che lui | parl*i* | ved*a* | sent*a* |
| che lei | parl*i* | ved*a* | sent*a* |
| che noi | parl*iamo* | ved*iamo* | sent*iamo* |
| che voi | parl*iate* | ved*iate* | sent*iate* |
| che loro | parl*ino* | ved*ano* | sent*ano* |

It is important in this tense to use the personal pronouns for the first three persons if the subject is unclear.

| Example: | Penso *che lui capisca.* | I think that he understands. |
|---|---|---|

The verbs in *-care* and *-gare* add an *h* in all forms of the present subjunctive.

Examples: **Giocare** (To play)       **Pagare** (To pay)

| che io | gio*chi* | che io | pag*hi* |
| che tu | gio*chi* | che io | pag*hi* |
| che lui | gio*chi* | che lui | pag*hi* |
| che lei | gio*chi* | che lei | pag*hi* |
| che noi | gio*chiamo* | che noi | pag*hiamo* |
| che voi | gio*chiate* | che voi | pag*hiate* |
| che loro | gio*chino* | che loro | pag*hino* |

The verbs in *-ciare* and *-giare* do not repeat the *i.*

Examples: **Cominciare** (To begin, start)       **Mangiare** (To eat)

| che io | cominc*i* | che io | mang*i* |
| che tu | cominc*i* | che tu | mang*i* |
| che lui | cominc*i* | che lui | mang*i* |
| che lei | cominc*i* | che lei | mang*i* |
| che noi | cominc*iamo* | che noi | mang*iamo* |
| che voi | cominc*iate* | che voi | mang*iate* |
| che loro | cominc*ino* | che loro | mang*ino* |

Verbs of the *-ire* conjugation with *isc* add an *-isc* between the root and the ending in all the singular persons and the 3rd person plural.

Example:       **Che + pronoun**       **Finire** (to finish)

| che io | fin*isca* |
| che tu | fin*isca* |
| che lui | fin*isca* |
| che lei | fin*isca* |
| che noi | fin*iamo* |
| che voi | fin*iate* |
| che loro | fin*iscano* |

The following commonly used verbs have irregular forms in the *present subjunctive.* All the endings have the vowel *a* regardless of whether they are *-are, -ere,* or *-ire* verbs.

| | |
|---|---|
| andare | *vada, vada, vada, andiamo, andiate, vadano* |
| avere | *abbia, abbia, abbia, abbiamo, abbiate, abbiano* |
| bere | *beva, beva, beva, beviamo, beviate, bevano* |
| dare | *dia, dia, dia, diamo, diate, diano* |
| dire | *dica, dica, dica, diciamo, diciate, dicano* |
| dovere | *debba, debba, debba, dobbiamo, dobbiate, debbano* |
| essere | *sia, sia, sia, siamo, siate, siano* |
| fare | *faccia, faccia, faccia, facciamo, facciate, facciano* |
| potere | *possa, possa, possa, possiamo, possiate, possano* |
| rimanere | *rimanga, rimanga, rimanga, rimaniamo, rimaniate, rimangano* |
| sapere | *sappia, sappia, sappia, sappiamo, sappiate, sappiano* |
| stare | *stia, stia, stia, stiamo, stiate, stiano* |
| uscire | *esca, esca, esca, usciamo, usciate, escano* |
| venire | *venga, venga, venga, veniamo, veniate, vengano* |
| volere | *voglia, voglia, voglia, vogliamo, vogliate, vogliano* |

## 3. The Subjunctive after Impersonal Expressions

The *present subjunctive* is used in a dependent *che* clause after impersonal expressions of possibility, opinion, and probability.

**Example:**    *È necessario che tu venga.*        It is necessary that you come.

Here are some impersonal expressions with which the subjunctive is used:

| | |
|---|---|
| *È necessario* | It is necessary |
| *È probabile* | It is probable |
| *È opportuno* | It is opportune |
| *È improbabile* | It is improbable |
| *È bene* | It is good |
| *È meglio* | It is better |
| *È giusto* | It is right |
| *È importante* | It is important |
| *È preferibile* | It is preferable |

If the impersonal verb indicates certainty, the subjunctive is not used.

**Example:**    *È certo che vengono oggi.*        It is certain they are coming today.

The impersonal expressions can also be followed by the infinitive with no subject indicated.

**Example:**    *È necessario studiare.*        It is necessary to study.

## 4. Practice

1. **domandare**    che io_____    che tu_____    che lui, lei_____
   (to ask)    che noi_____    che voi_____    che loro_____

2. **vedere**    che io_____    che tu_____    che lui, lei_____
   (to see)    che noi_____    che voi_____    che loro_____

3. **sentire**    che io_____    che tu_____    che lui, lei_____
   (to hear)    che noi_____    che voi_____    che loro_____

4. **capire**    che io_____    che tu_____    che lui, lei_____
   (to understand)    che noi_____    che voi_____    che loro_____

5. **giocare**    che io_____    che tu_____    che lui, lei_____
   (to play)    che noi_____    che voi_____    che loro_____

6. **pagare**    che io_____    che tu_____    che lui, lei_____
   (to pay)    che noi_____    che voi_____    che loro_____

## 5. Practice

Write the verbs in the *present subjunctive* in the person indicated.

**Che io:**

| domandare | decidere | sentire |
|---|---|---|
| _____ | _____ | _____ |

**Che tu:**

| comprare | vedere | finire |
|---|---|---|
| _____ | _____ | _____ |

**Che lui:**

| preparare | leggere | capire |
|---|---|---|
| _____ | _____ | _____ |

**Che lei:**

| aspettare | comprendere | pulire |
|---|---|---|
| _____ | _____ | _____ |

**Che noi:**

| arrivare | accendere | dire |
|---|---|---|
| _____ | _____ | _____ |

**Che voi:**

| visitare | bere | partire |
|---|---|---|
| _____ | _____ | _____ |

**Che loro:**

| lavorare | chiudere | capire |
|---|---|---|
| _____ | _____ | _____ |

# 6. Practice

Write the verbs in the *present subjunctive* in the person indicated or in the *infinitive.*

**Io voglio che tu:**

| mangiare | leggere | partire |
| --- | --- | --- |
| _____ | _____ | _____ |

**Io voglio che lui:**

| parlare | perdere | offrire |
| --- | --- | --- |
| _____ | _____ | _____ |

**Io voglio che lei:**

| stare | discutere | aprire |
| --- | --- | --- |
| _____ | _____ | _____ |

**Io spero che noi:**

| imparare | sorridere | capire |
| --- | --- | --- |
| _____ | _____ | _____ |

**Io desidero che voi:**

| fare | vedere | ridere |
| --- | --- | --- |
| _____ | _____ | _____ |

**Io penso che loro:**

| desiderare | dovere | ubbidire |
| --- | --- | --- |
| _____ | _____ | _____ |

**Io voglio:**

| visitare | vincere | capire |
| --- | --- | --- |
| _____ | _____ | _____ |

**Loro vogliono:**

| visitare | arrivare | partire |
| --- | --- | --- |
| _____ | _____ | _____ |

## 7. Practice

Choose the correct form of the verb from those in parentheses.

1. Mio padre vuole che io (legga, leggo) _____

2. Speriamo che i ragazzi (studiano, studino) _____

3. Spero che loro (comprano, comprino) _____

4. Penso che lui (capisce, capisca) _____

5. È necessario che io (vengo, venga) _____

6. È possibile che loro (arrivano, arrivino) _____

7. Vuole che tu (finisci, finisca) _____

8. Voglio che tu (vieni, venga) _____

9. Penso che tu (puoi, possa) _____

10. Credo che lui (legge, legga) _____

11. È bene che noi (veniamo, venire) _____

12. È possibile che voi (pensate, pensiate) _____

13. Credo di (sapere, sappia) _____

14. Spera che io (ritorni, ritorno) _____

15. Dubito che tu (sappia, so) _____

16. È bene che io (vado, vada) _____

17. Dubitiamo che lui (vince, vinca) _____

18. È possibile che lui (perda, perde) _____

19. È importante che loro (pensino, pensano) _____

20. È giusto che io (controlli, controllo) _____

21. È possibile che loro (possono, possano) _____

22. Ho voglia di (sapere, so) _____

23. Spero che loro (puliscano, puliscono) _____

24. Spera di (comprare, compri) _____

## 8. Practice

Change the verb from the *present indicative* to the *present subjunctive.*

1. Vado    _____

2. Sente (lui)    _____

3. Mangiamo    _____

4. Parlano    _____

5. Sentite    _____

6. Bevi    _____

7. Parte (lei)    _____

8. Capisce (lui)    _____

9. Lavoriamo    _____

10. Sentite    _____

11. Ascoltate    _____

12. Leggono    _____

13. Non ascoltate    _____

14. Andate    _____

15. Parto    _____

16. Arriva    _____

17. Piove    _____

18. So    _____

19. Conosci    _____

20. Puoi    _____

21. Non leggete    _____

22. Comprate    _____

23. Vendete    _____

24. Capite    _____

## 9. Practice

Rewrite the sentences, using the *present subjunctive* or *infinitive* of the verb in parentheses.

1.  Io voglio che tu (andare) _____

2.  Spero di (partire) _____

3.  Dubitiamo che lui (arrivare) _____

4.  Dubitiamo che lei (pensare) _____

5.  Speri che io (visitare) _____

6.  Speri di (andare) _____

7.  Speriamo che lui (capire) _____

8.  Speriamo di (comprare) _____

9.  Pensate che io (vedere) _____

10. Penso che tu (potere) _____

11. Pensi che noi (volere) _____

12. Dubito che tu (leggere) _____

13. Speriamo di (finire) _____

14. Sperano che io (pagare) _____

15. Carlo vuole che io (ascoltare) _____

16. Penso che Mario (comprare) _____

17. Pensa che noi (vendere) _____

18. Pensa che tu (scrivere) _____

19. Penso che loro (guardare) _____

20. Dubito che tu (studiare) _____

21. È necessario che lui (partire) _____

22. È possibile che noi (rimanere) _____

23. Ho paura che voi (perdere) _____

24. Voglio che tu (rimanere) _____

# Imperfect Subjunctive

## 10. Uses of the Imperfect Subjunctive

The imperfect subjunctive *(congiuntivo imperfetto),* like the present subjunctive, is used after certain verbs, impersonal expressions, and conjunctions. The main difference between these two tenses is the time of the action. If the action is in the present, the *present subjunctive* is used. If the action is related to the past, the *imperfect subjunctive* is used.

If the verb of the main clause is expressed in the past tense or conditional, the *imperfect subjunctive* is used in the dependent *che* clause.

**Example:**        Paola pensava che *io arrivassi.*        Paola thought I would arrive.

## 11. Forms of the Imperfect Subjunctive

The *imperfect subjunctive* of all regular verbs and almost all irregular verbs is formed by adding the endings *ssi, ssi, sse, ssimo, ste, ssero* to the 1st person singular of the imperfect indicative after omitting the final **vo.**

| Infinitive | Imperfect Indicative | Imperfect Subjunctive |
|---|---|---|
| Parlare | Parlavo | che io parlassi |
| Leggere | Leggevo | che io leggessi |
| Sentire | Sentivo | che io sentissi |

The following chart shows the forms of the *imperfect subjunctive* of the regular *-are, -ere, -ire* verbs.

|  | **Parlare** | **Scrivere** | **Sentire** |
|---|---|---|---|
| che io | parla*ssi* | scrive*ssi* | senti*ssi* |
| che tu | parla*ssi* | scrive*ssi* | senti*ssi* |
| che lui | parla*sse* | scrive*sse* | senti*sse* |
| che lei | parla*sse* | scrive*sse* | senti*sse* |
| che noi | parla*ssimo* | scrive*ssimo* | senti*ssimo* |
| che voi | parla*ste* | scrive*ste* | senti*ste* |
| che loro | parla*ssero* | scrive*ssero* | senti*ssero* |

The following verbs have *irregular* forms of the *imperfect subjunctive.*

| | |
|---|---|
| **stare** | *stessi, stessi, stesse, stessimo, steste, stessero* |
| **essere** | *fossi, fossi, fosse, fossimo, foste, fossero* |
| **dare** | *dessi, dessi, desse, dessimo, deste, dessero* |
| **dire** | *dicessi, dicessi, dicesse, dicessimo, diceste, dicessero* |
| **fare** | *facessi, facessi, facesse, facessimo, faceste, facessero* |

## 12. Practice

Write the *imperfect subjunctive* of the verbs.

1. **ascoltare**     che io_____   che tu_____   che lui, lei _____
   (to listen)     che noi_____   che voi_____   che loro _____

2. **conoscere**     che io_____   che tu_____   che lui, lei _____
   (to know)     che noi_____   che voi_____   che loro _____

3. **venire**     che io_____   che tu_____   che lui, lei _____
   (to come)     che noi_____   che voi_____   che loro _____

# 13. Practice

Write the verbs in the *imperfect subjunctive* in the person indicated.

**Che io:**

parlare                    leggere                    pulire

_____            _____            _____


**Che tu:**

comprare                   vedere                     finire

_____            _____            _____


**Che lui:**

andare                     potere                     sentire

_____            _____            _____


**Che lei:**

arrivare                   correre                    partire

_____            _____            _____


**Che noi:**

dimenticare                bere                       dormire

_____            _____            _____


**Che voi:**

perdonare                  scrivere                   venire

_____            _____            _____


**Che loro:**

studiare                   temere                     capire

_____            _____            _____

# 14. Practice

Write the verbs in the *imperfect subjunctive* in the person indicated.

**Pensavo che tu:**

fare                              vincere                           capire

_____        _____        _____


**Pensavo che lui:**

lavorare                          perdere                           finire

_____        _____        _____


**Pensavo che lei:**

studiare                          correggere                        sentire

_____        _____        _____


**Pensavo che noi:**

cambiare                          sapere                            dormire

_____        _____        _____


**Pensavo che voi:**

sognare                           accendere                         costruire

_____        _____        _____


**Pensavo che loro:**

insegnare                         spegnere                          venire

_____        _____        _____


**Speravo che tu:**

parlare                           vedere                            finire

_____        _____        _____


**Speravo che voi:**

fare                              leggere                           pulire

_____        _____        _____

## 15. Practice

Rewrite in Italian, using the *imperfect subjunctive*. Sometimes an *infinitive* will be needed.

1.  I wanted you (s.) to come _____

2.  I hoped you (s.) would come _____

3.  You thought you (s.) could study _____

4.  You (s.) thought he would study _____

5.  You (s.) thought we would come _____

6.  I hoped you (pl.) would come _____

7.  I believed he would write _____

8.  I thought we would go _____

9.  You (s.) hoped they would call _____

10. They thought I would remain _____

11. You all thought he would play _____

12. I thought you (s.) would clean _____

13. I did not know you (s.) would go _____

14. You (s.) wanted me to cook _____

15. She would like you (s.) to read _____

16. It would be necessary for you (s.) to leave _____

17. My father wanted me to work _____

18. It was difficult for you (s.) to go _____

19. I did not know you (s.) were so tall _____

20. She wanted me to ask the doctor _____

21. I wished to sleep all day long _____

22. I wished she slept all day long _____

23. He wanted us to go _____

24. I hoped they invited me _____

## 16. Practice

Change the verbs in parentheses to the *present subjunctive* or to the *imperfect subjunctive* as needed.

1.  Spero che tu (parlare) _____

2.  Speravo che tu (parlare) _____

3.  Dubito che noi (venire) _____

4.  Dubitavo che noi (venire) _____

5.  Pensiamo che lui (essere) _____

6.  Pensavamo che lui (essere) _____

7.  È probabile che io (studiare) _____

8.  Era probabile che lui (studiare) _____

9.  È necessario che voi (studiare) _____

10. Era necessario che voi (studiarc) _____

11. Credo di (venire) _____

12. Credevo di (venire) _____

13. Dubitiamo che lui (imparare) _____

14. Dubitavamo che lui (imparare) _____

15. Credo che tu (sognare) _____

16. Credeva che tu (sognare) _____

17. È possibile che loro (fare) _____

18. Era possibile che loro (fare) _____

19. Penso che voi (ricordare) _____

21. Spera che lui (arrivare) _____

22. Speravo che lui (arrivare) _____

23. Voglio che tu (scrivere) _____

24. Volevo che tu (scrivere) _____

# Chapter 8

## Past Subjunctive

### 1. Use of the Past Subjunctive

The past subjunctive *(congiuntivo passato)* is used in a dependent *che* clause to express the speaker's feelings toward a recent past action when the verb in the main clause is in the present indicative. The present of *avere* or *essere* and the *past participle* of the verb are used.

**Example:**     Credo che *abbiano vinto* la partita.     I think that they won the game.

Note that the action in the *che* clause is in the past in relation to the action in the main clause, which is in the present tense.

### 2. Forms of the Past Subjunctive

The following chart shows the conjugations of *trovare, vedere, partire* in the past subjunctive.

|  | **Trovare** (To find) | **Credere** (To believe) | **Sentire** (To hear) |
|---|---|---|---|
| *che io* | abbia trovato | abbia creduto | abbia sentito |
| *che tu* | abbia trovato | abbia creduto | abbia sentito |
| *che lui* | abbia trovato | abbia creduto | abbia sentito |
| *che lei* | abbia trovato | abbia creduto | abbia sentito |
| *che noi* | abbiamo trovato | abbiamo creduto | abbiamo sentito |
| *che voi* | abbiate trovato | abbiate creduto | abbiate sentito |
| *che loro* | abbiano trovato | abbiano creduto | abbiano sentito |

**Conjugation of the past subjunctive using** *essere*

Partire (To leave, to depart)

| *che io* | sia partito/a |
|---|---|
| *che tu* | sia partito/a |
| *che lui* | sia partito |
| *che lei* | sia partita |
| *che noi* | siamo partiti/e |
| *che voi* | siate partiti/e |
| *che loro* | siano partiti/e |

## 3. Practice

Write the *past subjunctive* of the verbs in the person indicated.

**Che io:**

arrivare

_____

vedere

_____

finire

_____

**Che tu:**

parlare

_____

leggere

_____

capire

_____

**Che lui:**

ascoltare

_____

scrivere

_____

sentire

_____

**Che lei:**

piantare

_____

scendere

_____

salire

_____

**Che noi:**

studiare

_____

vendere

_____

sostituire

_____

**Che voi:**

cancellare

_____

bere

_____

venire

_____

**Che loro:**

guardare

_____

mantenere

_____

partire

_____

**Che io:**

non sperare

_____

non aspettare

_____

non ridere

_____

# 4. Practice

Complete the sentences with the *past subjunctive.*

1. È bene che Paolo (venire) _____

2. Speriamo che lui (parlare) _____

3. Loro sono contenti che noi (studiare) _____

4. Mi dispiace che tu (perdere) _____

5. Sono contento che noi (andare) _____

6. È giusto che lui (pagare) _____

7. È possibile che la polizia (arrestare) _____

8. Ci dispiace che tu non (trovare) _____

9. Ci dispiace che voi non (mangiare) _____

10. È bene che Maria (partire) _____

11. Sono sorpreso che lui (telefonare) _____

12. È sorpreso che voi (telefonare) _____

13. È possibile che lei non (studiare) _____

14. Spero che loro (venire) _____

15. Spero che voi (nuotare) _____

16. È giusto che io (ritornare) _____

17. È impossibile che lui (finire) _____

18. Siamo contenti che lui (capire) _____

19. Non credo che tu (trovare) _____

20. È possibile che Carlo (partire) _____

21. È necessario che tu (scrivere) _____

22. Siamo contenti che loro (studiare) _____

23. Sono sorpreso che tu (studiare) _____

24. Ci dispiace che lui non (telefonare) _____

# 5. Practice

Write the verbs in three forms of the *subjunctive: present, imperfect, past.*

| Present | Imperfect | Past |
|---|---|---|
| 1. Che io parlare | | |
| 2. Che tu sentire | | |
| 3. Che lui capire | | |
| 4. Che lei venire | | |
| 5. Che noi offrire | | |
| 6. Che voi prendere | | |
| 7. Che loro vedere | | |
| 8. Che io non pensare | | |
| 9. Che tu non leggere | | |
| 10. Che lui non pulire | | |
| 11. Che noi non stare | | |

# Pluperfect Subjunctive

## 6. Use of the Pluperfect Subjunctive

The pluperfect subjunctive *(congiuntivo trapassato)* is used when the action of the verb in the dependent clause happened before the action of the verb in the main clause, which is in the past.

It is formed by the imperfect subjunctive of *essere* and *avere* plus the *past participle* of the verb.

**Example:**

| Pres. Ind. | Perfect Subj. | Imp. Ind. | Pluperfect Subj. |
|---|---|---|---|
| *Credo che Mario sia venuto.* | | *Credevo che Mario fosse venuto.* | |
| I think that Mario came. | | I thought that Mario had come. | |

## 7. Forms of the Pluperfect Subjunctive

The following chart shows the conjugations of the *pluperfect subjunctive* with *essere* and *avere*.

| | Partire | Capire |
|---|---|---|
| *che io* | *fossi partito/a* | *avessi capito* |
| *che tu* | *fossi partito/a* | *avessi capito* |
| *che lui/lei* | *fosse partito/a* | *avesse capito* |
| *che noi* | *fossimo partiti/e* | *avessimo capito* |
| *che voi* | *foste partiti/e* | *aveste capito* |
| *che loro* | *fossero partiti/e* | *avessero capito* |

## 8. Practice

Rewrite in English.

1. Che io fossi arrivato _____

2. Che tu avessi pensato _____

3. Che noi fossimo partiti _____

4. Che voi aveste parlato _____

5. Che loro fossero venuti _____

# 9. Practice

Rewrite the sentences, using the *imperfect subjunctive* in the main clause and the *pluperfect subjunctive* in the *che* clause.

1. Sembra che sappia tutto (lui) _____

2. È possibile che arrivi (lei) _____

3. Speriamo che entri (lei) _____

4. Penso che lui arrivi _____

5. Dubito che sappia (tu) _____

6. Sembra che capisca (lui) _____

7. È meglio che tu vada _____

8. È meglio che loro partano _____

9. Sembra che io sappia _____

10. Preferisco che voi andiate _____

11. Preferiamo che tu studi _____

12. Sono sicuro che Carlo arrivi _____

13. Preferisce che impariamo _____

14. Sono contento che tu venga _____

15. Siamo sicuri che partano _____

16. È probabile che tu arrivi _____

17. Penso che tu venga _____

18. Dubito che lui trovi lavoro _____

19. Credo che lei cerchi lavoro _____

20. È necessario che io legga _____

21. È bene che loro comprino _____

22. È necessario che vendano _____

23. Spero che Carlo venda _____

# *Se* Clauses and the Subjunctive

## 10. Contrary-to-Fact

To express a *contrary-to-fact* statement in the present or the future, the *imperfect subjunctive* is used in the *se clause.* The conditional is normally used in the main clause to express a conclusion to the action.

**Example:**     *Se potessi,* verrei.          If I could, I would come.

To express a contrary-to-fact statement in the past, the pluperfect subjunctive is used in the *se clause* and the past conditional is used in the main clause.

**Example:**     *Se avessi saputo, sarei venuto.*     If I had known, I would have come.

## 11. Wishes

*Se* + the *imperfect subjunctive* is used in exclamations to express wishes that may never materialize.

**Examples:**     *Se avessi* tanti soldi!          If only I had a lot of money!
                  *Se potessi* parlare!          If only I could talk!

## 12. Practice

Use the verbs in parentheses in the correct tense of the subjunctive.

1.  Capirei se tu (spiegare) _____

2.  Studieresti se (potere) _____

3.  Compreremmo se (avere) i soldi _____

4.  Scriverebbe se (sapere) _____

5.  Verrebbe se (guidare) _____

6.  Avrebbe capito se tu (spiegare) _____

7.  Avrebbe studiato se (potere) _____

8.  Avremmo comprato se (avere) soldi _____

9.  Avrebbe scritto se (sapere) _____

10. Sarebbe venuto se (guidare) _____

11. Avresti comprato se lui (vendere) _____

12. Sarei andato se (sapere) _____

13. Avresti parlato se tu (potere) _____

14. Avreste capito se voi (studiare) _____

# Reflexive Verbs

## 13. The Nature of Reflexive Verbs

A reflexive verb *(verbo riflessivo)* is one in which the object of the verb is the same person or thing as the subject. They are more common in Italian than in English.

| Examples: | *Mi pettino.* | I comb my hair. |
| | *Mi sveglio* presto. | I wake up early. |
| | Carlo *si diverte.* | Carlo enjoys himself. |

Some Italian verbs have both reflexive and nonreflexive forms.

| Examples: | Noi *laviamo* tutti i giorni. | We wash every day. |
| | Noi *ci laviamo* tutti i giorni. | We wash ourselves every day. |

Plural reflexive verbs used with the reflexive pronouns *ci, vi,* and *si* express a reciprocal meaning.

| Example: | *Ci vediamo* ogni lunedì. | We see each other every Monday. |
| | *Si scrivono* spesso. | They write each other often. |

**Note:** In Italian, the *reflexive* is often used where English uses an impersonal construction or the passive.

| Examples: | Qui *si parla* italiano. | Here one speaks Italian. |
| | Come *si va* alla stazione? | How do you go to the station? |
| | Come *si fa* la pizza? | How do you make pizza? |

## 14. Forms of Reflexive Verbs

In the present tense, the reflexive pronoun comes before the verb, but in the infinitive it is attached to the end, with the final *e* of the infinitive dropped.

| Examples: | *Mi lavo* subito. | I wash myself right away. |
| | Vado a *lavarmi* subito. | I'm going to wash myself right away. |

In the passato prossimo, reflexive verbs always use the auxiliary *essere* and a past participle that agrees with the subject.

| Examples: | Giovanni *si è* addormentato. | Giovanni fell asleep. |
| | Carla *si è* addormentata. | Carla fell asleep. |

Following is the conjugation of the present tense of *alzarsi*. The other tenses follow the same patterns of the regular verbs with the exception of the pronoun, which has to be placed in front of the verb.

| **Alzarsi** | | | To get up |
|---|---|---|---|
| *io* | *mi* | *alzo* | I get up |
| *tu* | *ti* | *alzi* | you get up |
| *lui* | *si* | *alza* | he gets up |
| *lei* | *si* | *alza* | she gets up |
| *noi* | *ci* | *alziamo* | we get up |
| *voi* | *vi* | *alzate* | you get up |
| *loro* | *si* | *alzano* | they get up |

## 15. List of Common Reflexive Verbs

Here is a list of some common reflexive verbs in Italian. They are not necessarily reflexive in English.

| | |
|---|---|
| **addormentarsi** | to fall asleep |
| **aiutarsi** | to help one another |
| **alzarsi** | to get up |
| **amarsi** | to love each other |
| **chiamarsi** | to be called |
| **divertirsi** | to enjoy oneself, to have a good time |
| **incontrarsi** | to meet each other |
| **innamorarsi** | to fall in love |
| **lavarsi** | to wash oneself |
| **mettersi** | to put on (clothing) |
| **mettersi a** | to start, to begin |
| **odiarsi** | to hate one another |
| **parlarsi** | to speak to each other |
| **prepararsi** | to get ready |
| **salutarsi** | to greet one another |
| **scriversi** | to write each other |
| **sentirsi** | to feel |
| **svegliarsi** | to wake up |
| **vedersi** | to see each other |
| **vestirsi** | to get dressed |

# 16. Practice

Write the verbs in the present indicative in the person indicated.

**Io:**

| alzarsi | mettersi | sentirsi |
|---|---|---|
| _____ | _____ | _____ |

**Tu:**

| addormentarsi | pettinarsi | domandarsi |
|---|---|---|
| _____ | _____ | _____ |

**Lui:**

| lavarsi | pettinarsi | vestirsi |
|---|---|---|
| _____ | _____ | _____ |

**Lei:**

| divertirsi | sposarsi | prepararsi |
|---|---|---|
| _____ | _____ | _____ |

**Noi:**

| vestirsi | svegliarsi | aiutarsi |
|---|---|---|
| _____ | _____ | _____ |

**Voi:**

| parlarsi | salutarsi | incontrarsi |
|---|---|---|
| _____ | _____ | _____ |

**Loro:**

| divertirsi | sposarsi | prepararsi |
|---|---|---|
| _____ | _____ | _____ |

# 17. Practice

Rewrite in English.

1. Si sveglia (lui) _____

2. Lei si veste _____

3. Loro si preparano _____

4. Ci prepariamo _____

5. Vi salutate _____

6. Si parlano _____

7. Vi odiate _____

8. Si amano _____

9. Si mette a parlare _____

10. Si scrivono _____

11. Mi alzo _____

12. Ti lavi _____

13. Si lava (lui) _____

14. Carlo si veste _____

15. Ci incontriamo _____

16. Mi vesto _____

17. Si addormenta _____

18. Vi parlate _____

19. Si aiutano _____

20. Mi addormento _____

21. Si pettina (lui) _____

22. Si specchiano _____

23. Vi preparate _____

24. Si inginocchiano _____

## 18. Practice

Rewrite in Italian.

1. We wake up _____

2. I enjoy myself _____

3. They get up _____

4. They wake up _____

5. They greet each other _____

6. They get ready _____

7. He washes himself _____

8. She combs her hair _____

9. They meet each other _____

10. They enjoy themselves _____

11. She enjoys herself _____

12. He gets ready _____

13. You (pl.) get dressed _____

14. I get dressed _____

15. We help each other _____

16. We get up _____

17. We wake up _____

18. We love each other _____

19. We woke up _____

20. He got up _____

21. You (s.) washed yourself _____

22. She combed her hair _____

23. They hated each other _____

24. He enjoyed himself _____

# Chapter 9

## Progressive Tenses

### 1. Uses of the Progressive Tenses

In Italian, often the present and the imperfect tenses are used to express continuing actions, while in English the progressive tenses are generally used.

| | | |
|---|---|---|
| **Examples:** | *Mangiano.* | *They are eating.* |
| | *Scrivo* una lettera di affari. | *I am writing* a business letter. |
| | *Parlavano.* | *They were talking.* |

In Italian, the progressive tense is used when one wants to emphasize that the action is going on at the time of speaking.

There are two progressive tenses: *present progressive* and *past progressive.*

| | | |
|---|---|---|
| **Present Progressive:** | Dove *stai andando?* | Where are you going? |
| **Past Progressive:** | Dove *stavi andando?* | Where were you going? |

### 2. Forms of the Progressive

The progressive tenses are formed with the verb *stare* + the *gerund.* The gerund is formed by adding *-ando, -endo, -endo* forms to the infinitive stem of *-are, -ere,* and *-ire* verbs respectively.

| | | |
|---|---|---|
| **Examples:** | parlare | *parlando* |
| | tenere | *tenendo* |
| | sentire | *sentendo* |

The present of *stare* is used for the *present progressive,* and the imperfect of *stare* is used for the *past progressive.*

Following are the complete conjugations of the *present progressive* and the *past progressive*.

**Present Progressive**

| | | |
|---|---|---|
| io | **sto** | *parlando (I am speaking)* |
| tu | **stai** | *parlando* |
| lui | **sta** | *parlando* |
| lei | **sta** | *parlando* |
| noi | **stiamo** | *parlando* |
| voi | **state** | *parlando* |
| loro | **stanno** | *parlando* |

**Past Progressive**

| | | |
|---|---|---|
| io | **stavo** | *parlando (I was speaking)* |
| tu | **stavi** | *parlando* |
| lui | **stava** | *parlando* |
| lei | **stava** | *parlando* |
| noi | **stavamo** | *parlando* |
| voi | **stavate** | *parlando* |
| loro | **stavano** | *parlando* |

**Note:** Reflexive pronouns may precede or follow *stare*.

**Example:**  Lei *si sta pettinando.*     She is combing her hair.

or

Lei *sta pettinandosi.*     She is combing her hair.

## 3. Practice

Change the present tense into the *present progressive* and the imperfect to the *past progressive*.

**A.**

1. Io parlo _____

2. Tu ascolti _____

3. Noi parliamo_____

4. Lui guida _____

5. Lei sente _____

6. Noi studiamo _____

7. Voi partite_____

8. Tu leggi _____

9. Lei parla _____

10. Io gioco_____

11. Tu parti _____

12. Loro tornano_____

**B.**

1. Tu andavi _____

2. Tu ascoltavi _____

3. Voi parlavate _____

4. Io bevevo _____

5. Voi vedevate_____

6. Noi giocavamo_____

7. Voi scrivevate_____

8. Lui leggeva _____

9. Tu prendevi _____

10. Io bevevo _____

11. Tu partivi _____

12. Io tornavo _____

# Modal Verbs

## 4. Common Modal Verbs

A *modal verb* is a special verb usually followed by an infinitive. The common modal verbs are:

*dovere* (must, to have to, should)       expresses duty
*potere* (to be able to, can)      expresses ability
*volere* (to want)      expresses wants

*Devo* studiare.      I must (have to) study.
*Possono* rimanere.      They can stay.
*Vogliamo* pagare.      We want to pay.

**Note:** All *modal verbs* are sometimes used without the infinitive, mainly in responses.

> **Examples:**      *Puoi leggere* un po'?      Can you read a little?
> No, non *posso.*      No, I can't.

The modal verbs are conjugated with **avere** in the compound tenses when the infinitive following the modal verb is transitive, with **essere** if the infinitive is intransitive.

> **Examples:**      Maria *ha dovuto* pagare.      Mary had to pay.
> Maria *è dovuta andare* a pagare.      Mary had to go to pay.

## 5. Forms of the Modal Verbs

|  | **Dovere** | **Volere** | **Potere** |
|---|---|---|---|
| *Present:* | devo | voglio | posso |
|  | devi | vuoi | puoi |
|  | deve | vuole | può |
|  | dobbiamo | vogliamo | possiamo |
|  | dovete | volete | potete |
|  | devono | vogliono | possono |
| *Future:* | dovrò | vorrò | potrò |
|  | dovrai | vorrai | potrai |
|  | dovrà | vorrà | potrà |
|  | dovremo | vorremo | potremo |
|  | dovrete | vorrete | potrete |
|  | dovranno | vorranno | potranno |
| *Imperf.:* | dovevo | volevo | potevo |
|  | dovevi | volevi | potevi |
|  | etc. | etc. | etc. |

|  | **Dovere** | **Volere** | **Potere** |
|---|---|---|---|
| **Passato Prossimo:** | ho (sono) dovuto<br>hai (sei) dovuto<br>etc. | ho (sono) voluto<br>hai (sei) voluto<br>etc. | ho (sono) potuto<br>hai (sei) potuto<br>etc. |
| **Present Condit.:** | dovrei<br>dovresti<br>dovrebbe<br>dovremmo<br>dovreste<br>dovrebbero | vorrei<br>vorresti<br>vorrebbe<br>vorremmo<br>vorreste<br>vorrebbero | potrei<br>potresti<br>potrebbe<br>potremmo<br>potreste<br>potrebbero |
| **Past Condit.:** | avrei (sarei) dovuto<br>avresti (saresti)<br>dovuto<br>etc. | avrei (sarei) voluto<br>avresti (saresti)<br>voluto<br>etc. | avrei (sarei) potuto<br>avresti (saresti)<br>potuto<br>etc. |
| **Present Subjunct.:** | che io, tu, lui debba<br>che noi dobbiamo<br>che voi dobbiate<br>che loro debbano | che io, tu, lui voglia<br>che noi vogliamo<br>che voi vogliate<br>che loro vogliano | che io, tu, lui possa<br>che noi possiamo<br>che voi possiate<br>che loro possano |
| **Imperfect Subjunct.:** | dovessi<br>dovessi<br>dovesse<br>dovessimo<br>doveste<br>dovessero | volessi<br>volessi<br>volesse<br>volessimo<br>voleste<br>volessero | potessi<br>potessi<br>potesse<br>potessimo<br>poteste<br>potessero |
| **Past Subjunct.:** | avessi (fossi) dovuto<br>avessi (fossi) dovuto<br>avesse (fosse) dovuto<br>etc. | avessi (fossi) voluto<br>avessi (fossi) voluto<br>avesse (fosse) voluto<br>etc. | avessi (fossi) potuto<br>avessi (fossi) potuto<br>avesse (fosse) potuto<br>etc. |

**Note:** When *dovere, volere, potere* are conjugated with the verb *essere,* the past participle of the verb agrees in gender and number with the subject.

## 6. Practice

Rewrite in English.

Voglio andare

_____

Devo studiare

_____

Posso portare

_____

Volevamo partire

_____

Dovevamo arrivare

_____

Potevamo sentire

_____

Vorrà portare

_____

Dovrà correre

_____

Potrà comprare

_____

Hanno voluto ascoltare

_____

Hanno dovuto fare

_____

Hanno potuto dire

_____

Sono voluti venire

_____

Sono dovuti andare

_____

Sono potuti partire

_____

## 7. Practice

Rewrite in Italian.

I want to think

_____

I must go

_____

I can sing

_____

You (s.) wanted to write

_____

You (s.) had to see

_____

You (s.) could sell (past)

_____

We would like to come

_____

We should buy

_____

We could read (possibility)

_____

They have wanted to play

_____

They have had to close

_____

They could have cleaned

_____

# The Passive Voice

In the *active voice* studied so far, the subject performs the action. In the *passive voice,* the subject receives the action.

| | | |
|---|---|---|
| **Examples:** | ***Active Voice*** | ***Passive Voice*** |
| | Maria *cucina* la cena. | La cena *è cucinata* da Maria. |
| | Mary *cooks* dinner. | Dinner *is cooked* by Mary. |
| | Maria *ha cucinato* la cena | La cena *è stata cucinata* da Maria. |
| | Mary *cooked* dinner. | The dinner *was cooked* by Mary. |

The *passive* in Italian is formed as in English, with the verb *essere* and the *past participle* of the verb needed. The past participle agrees with the subject in gender and number. The reflexive form is used instead of the *passive* in Italian when the person doing the action is not mentioned.

| | | |
|---|---|---|
| **Examples:** | La lettera *fu spedita* | The letter was mailed |
| | ieri da mio padre. | yesterday by my father. |
| | *Si sono spedite* le lettere ieri. | The letters were mailed yesterday. |

## 8. Practice

Rewrite in English.

1. Quando è stato pagato il conto?  _____

2. Da chi è stata scritta la Divina Commedia?  _____

3. L'America è stata scoperta nel 1492.  _____

4. Il ragazzo è stato svegliato.  _____

5. La casa è finita.  _____

## 9. Practice

Rewrite in Italian.

1. English is studied by many.  _____

2. The game was played in the rain.  _____

3. When was the dog found?  _____

4. The house is cleaned by Paul.  _____

5. The car was sold quickly.  _____

# Verbs That Follow Common Patterns

Many verbs in Italian are conjugated like other irregular verbs. By knowing the common verbs, you can conjugate many other verbs. Study these examples.

### Dire

| | |
|---|---|
| *benedire* | to bless |
| *contraddire* | to contradict |
| *disdire* | to retract |
| *maledire* | to curse |
| *interdire* | to forbid |
| *predire* | to predict |

### Fare

| | |
|---|---|
| *assuefarsi* | to get accustomed |
| *contraffare* | to imitate |
| *disfare* | to undo |
| *rifare* | to redo |
| *soddisfare* | to satisfy |
| *stupefare* | to amaze |

### Porre

| | |
|---|---|
| *deporre* | to put down |
| *opporre* | to oppose |
| *proporre* | to propose |
| *supporre* | to suppose |

### Prendere

| | |
|---|---|
| *contendere* | to compete, to quarrel |
| *distendere* | to relax |
| *estendere* | to extend |
| *fraintendere* | to misunderstand |
| *pretendere* | to claim |

### Vedere

| | |
|---|---|
| *avvedersi* | to become aware |
| *intravedere* | to glimpse |
| *prevedere* | to foresee |
| *rivedere* | to see again, to review |

### Venire

| | |
|---|---|
| *addivenire* | to come to an agreement |
| *divenire* | to become |
| *intervenire* | to intervene |
| *pervenire* | to reach |
| *prevenire* | to anticipate |

### Cogliere

| | |
|---|---|
| *distogliere* | to dissuade |
| *raccogliere* | to gather |
| *togliere* | to remove |

### Tenere

| | |
|---|---|
| *attenersi* | to keep, to stick to |
| *contenere* | to contain |
| *ottenere* | to obtain |

# 10. Practice

Write the verbs in the tense and person indicated.

## Present

1. io (disdire) _____
2. tu (rifare) _____
3. voi (fraintendere) _____
4. loro (intervenire) _____
5. io (togliere)_____

6. lei (rifare) _____
7. loro (supporre) _____
8. lui (ottenere)_____
9. loro (interdire) _____
10. noi (rivedere) _____

## Future

1. io (rifare) _____
2. loro (contendere) _____
3. lui (supporrc) _____
4. noi (prevedere) _____
5. voi (rifare) _____

6. noi (opporre) _____
7. loro (ottenere)_____
8. io (prcdirc) _____
9. lei (contraddire) _____
10. loro (intervenire) _____

## Passato Remoto

1. loro (addivenire)_____
2. lui (prevedere) _____
3. loro (soddisfare)_____
4. noi (predire) _____
5. io (togliere)_____

6. voi (fraintendere) _____
7. lei (proporre) _____
8. loro (contraddire) _____
9. tu (prevenire) _____
10. loro (contraffare) _____

## Passato Prossimo

1. io (stupefare) _____
2. tu (opporre) _____
3. noi (disdire) _____

4. loro (prevedere) _____
5. lei (ottenere) _____
6. tu (pretendere) _____

## 11. Practice

Rewrite in Italian. Use the *present, future,* or *passato remoto*.

1. They predicted _____

2. We'll relax _____

3. He becomes _____

4. We'll reach _____

5. She'll forbid _____

6. They supposed _____

7. They imitate _____

8. We anticipate _____

9. He'll foresee _____

10. You (s.) oppose _____

11. They'll satisfy _____

12. You (pl.) misunderstand _____

13. She gathered _____

14. You (s.) contradict _____

15. We competed _____

16. I'll remove _____

17. They'll amaze _____

18. He became aware _____

19. I redo _____

20. You relaxed _____

21. We suppose _____

22. I proposed _____

23. We dissuade _____

24. She gathers _____

25. I'll retract _____

26. We'll imitate _____

27. You (s.) oppose _____

28. You (pl.) became _____

29. We removed _____

30. She intervened _____

# Chapter 10

## General Review of Verbs

### 1. Present

Write the verbs in the *present indicative* in the person indicated.

**Io:**

| parlare | vedere | sentire | capire |
|---|---|---|---|
| | | | |

**Tu:**

| camminare | scrivere | partire | finire |
|---|---|---|---|
| | | | |

**Lui:**

| lavorare | leggere | venire | pulire |
|---|---|---|---|
| | | | |

**Lei:**

| cucinare | temere | dire | uscire |
|---|---|---|---|
| | | | |

**Noi:**

| insegnare | volere | scoprire | offrire |
|---|---|---|---|
| | | | |

**Voi:**

| arrivare | vincere | avvenire | riuscire |
|---|---|---|---|
| | | | |

**Loro:**

| cambiare | perdere | morire | salire |
|---|---|---|---|
| | | | |

## 2. Imperfect

Write the verbs in the *imperfect* in the person indicated.

| | | | |
|---|---|---|---|
| io cominciare | tu parlare | lui arrivare | lei mangiare |
| | | | |
| lui perdere | lei vincere | noi dire | loro dare |
| | | | |
| noi venire | tu capire | lei finire | io salire |
| | | | |
| io parlare | tu diventare | lei comprare | noi passare |
| | | | |
| tu leggere | noi essere | voi scrivere | loro dovere |
| | | | |
| noi finire | voi dire | loro capire | tu finire |
| | | | |
| io chiudere | tu arrivare | lui partire | lei uscire |
| | | | |
| noi cambiare | voi scrivere | loro entrare | tu fuggire |
| | | | |
| io avere | tu dovere | noi andare | lui essere |
| | | | |
| noi potere | tu fare | lei uscire | loro volere |
| | | | |
| loro venire | lei dire | loro uscire | lei finire |
| | | | |
| io andare | loro capire | voi finire | tu partire |

## 3. Future

**A.** Rewrite in English.

1. Mangerò _____
2. Sentirai _____
3. Salirà (lui) _____
4. Compreremo _____
5. Faremo _____
6. Studierò _____
7. Sentirò _____
8. Ascolterà _____
9. Partirete _____
10. Capirete _____
11. Farò _____
12. Vorrai _____
13. Dovrete _____
14. Vi alzerete _____
15. Guiderò _____
16. Voleremo _____
17. Fermerai _____
18. Saprò _____
19. Conoscerò _____
20. Arriveremo _____
21. Starò _____
22. Saremo _____
23. Leggerete _____

**B.** Rewrite in Italian.

1. I will go _____
2. You will sleep _____
3. He will eat _____
4. I will clean _____
5. She will walk _____
6. You (pl.) will call _____
7. I will listen _____
8. You (s.) will change _____
9. We will stay _____
10. They will enter _____
11. I will laugh _____
12. We will be able _____
13. I will see _____
14. You (pl.) will go _____
15. They will write _____
16. He will answer _____
17. I will have to _____
18. I will forget _____
19. She will clean _____
20. They will stay _____
21. I will do _____
22. She will close _____
23. They will drink _____

## 4. Passato Remoto and Passato Prossimo

Change the infinitive first into the *passato remoto,* then into the *passato prossimo.*

|  | Passato Remoto | Passato Prossimo |
|---|---|---|
| **Io:**<br>andare | _____ | _____ |
| **Tu:**<br>fare | _____ | _____ |
| **Lui:**<br>venire | _____ | _____ |
| **Lei:**<br>capire | _____ | _____ |
| **Noi:**<br>vedere | _____ | _____ |
| **Voi:**<br>pensare | _____ | _____ |
| **Loro:**<br>sentire | _____ | _____ |
| **Io:**<br>stare | _____ | _____ |
| **Tu:**<br>chiedere | _____ | _____ |
| **Lui:**<br>mandare | _____ | _____ |
| **Lei:**<br>pensare | _____ | _____ |

# 5. Trapassato Prossimo

**A.** Rewrite in English.

1. Avevo mangiato _____

2. Avevamo capito _____

3. Avevano dormito _____

4. Erano partiti _____

5. Ero andato _____

6. Eravamo stati _____

7. Avevamo parlato _____

8. Avevi studiato _____

9. Avevo capito _____

10. Avevo chiuso _____

11. Avevi sentito _____

12. Avevamo portato _____

13. Aveva perso (lui) _____

14. Avevate vinto _____

15. Avevo telefonato _____

16. Aveva finito (lei) _____

17. Ero stato _____

18. Erano saliti _____

19. Era scesa (lei) _____

20. Eravate partiti _____

21. Eravamo dispiaciute _____

22. Erano morti _____

23. Ero entrata _____

**B.** Rewrite in Italian, using the *trapassato prossimo.*

1. I had slept _____

2. He had entered _____

3. She had spoken _____

4. We had understood _____

5. You (pl.) had made _____

6. He had done _____

7. She had written _____

8. You (s.) had been _____

9. She had seen _____

10. We had come _____

11. They had returned _____

12. We had gone _____

13. I had eaten _____

14. You (s.) had written _____

15. They had cleaned _____

16. We had read _____

17. She had put _____

18. We had told _____

19. I had known _____

20. He had seen _____

21. I had wanted _____

22. You (pl.) had said _____

23. She was born _____

# 6. Present Conditional

Rewrite in Italian, using the *present conditional.*

1.  I would like      _____

2.  I would read      _____

3.  You (pl.) would speak      _____

4.  She would listen      _____

5.  I would clean      _____

6.  They would write      _____

7.  We would think      _____

8.  I would answer      _____

9.  You (s.) would read      _____

10.  He would eat      _____

11.  She would sell      _____

12.  We would study      _____

13.  I would ski      _____

14.  They would travel      _____

15.  You (pl.) would drink      _____

16.  I would study      _____

17.  I should      _____

18.  I could      _____

19.  You (s.) would want      _____

20.  We would think      _____

21.  They would close      _____

22.  We would open      _____

23.  She would understand      _____

## 7. Past Conditional

Rewrite in Italian, using the *past conditional.*

1. I would have liked _____

2. I would have been _____

3. She would have spoken _____

4. I would have listened _____

5. You (pl.) would have cleaned _____

6. They would have written _____

7. They would have thought _____

8. He would have read _____

9. We would have eaten _____

10. They would have arrived _____

11. I would have been _____

12. We would have stayed _____

13. You (s.) would have drunk _____

14. He would have studied _____

15. She would have gone _____

16. You (pl.) would have wanted _____

17. I would have closed _____

18. He would have opened _____

19. She would have thought _____

20. We would have understood _____

21. They would have traveled _____

22. You (s.) would have sung _____

23. They would have looked _____

24. We would have come _____

## 8. Present Subjunctive and Imperfect Subjunctive

Change the infinitive to the *present* and *imperfect subjunctive* in the person indicated.

| | **Present Subjunctive** | **Imperfect Subjunctive** |
|---|---|---|
| 1. Che io mangiare | _____ | _____ |
| 2. Che tu vedere | _____ | _____ |
| 3. Che lui parlare | _____ | _____ |
| 4. Che lei sentire | _____ | _____ |
| 5. Che noi chiudere | _____ | _____ |
| 6. Che voi capire | _____ | _____ |
| 7. Che loro venire | _____ | _____ |
| 8. Che noi rispondere | _____ | _____ |
| 9. Che tu scrivere | _____ | _____ |
| 10. Che io imparare | _____ | _____ |
| 11. Che lui finire | _____ | _____ |
| 12. Che noi mangiare | _____ | _____ |
| 13. Che voi bere | _____ | _____ |
| 14. Che loro sapere | _____ | _____ |
| 15. Che tu telefonare | _____ | _____ |
| 16. Che lei prendere | _____ | _____ |
| 17. Che voi stare | _____ | _____ |
| 18. Che io stare | _____ | _____ |
| 19. Che voi dovere | _____ | _____ |
| 20. Che loro capire | _____ | _____ |
| 21. Che lei leggere | _____ | _____ |
| 22. Che tu mandare | _____ | _____ |
| 23. Che lui vendere | _____ | _____ |

## 9. Past Subjunctive and Pluperfect Subjunctive

Change the following verbs to the *past subjunctive* and *pluperfect subjunctive.*

|  | Past Subjunctive | Pluperfect Subjunctive |
|---|---|---|
| 1. Che io venire | _____ | _____ |
| 2. Che lui parlare | _____ | _____ |
| 3. Che noi ascoltare | _____ | _____ |
| 4. Che lei fare | _____ | _____ |
| 5. Che voi finire | _____ | _____ |
| 6. Che voi andare | _____ | _____ |
| 7. Che loro chiudere | _____ | _____ |
| 8. Che tu aprire | _____ | _____ |
| 9. Che io potere | _____ | _____ |
| 10. Che lei dire | _____ | _____ |
| 11. Che noi finire | _____ | _____ |
| 12. Che tu capire | _____ | _____ |
| 13. Che io rispondere | _____ | _____ |
| 14. Che lei vedere | _____ | _____ |
| 15. Che voi parlare | _____ | _____ |
| 16. Che io vivere | _____ | _____ |
| 17. Che lei prendere | _____ | _____ |
| 18. Che loro viaggiare | _____ | _____ |
| 19. Che io ordinare | _____ | _____ |
| 20. Che voi insegnare | _____ | _____ |
| 21. Che tu bere | _____ | _____ |
| 22. Che lei aspettare | _____ | _____ |
| 23. Che tu ricevere | _____ | _____ |

## 10. Present, Future, Imperfect, Passato Remoto

Change the following verbs to the tense and person indicated.

| | Present | Future | Imperfect | Passato Remoto |
|---|---|---|---|---|
| Io fare | | | | |
| Tu andare | | | | |
| Lui mangiare | | | | |
| Lei parlare | | | | |
| Noi leggere | | | | |
| Voi bere | | | | |
| Loro vedere | | | | |
| Io sentire | | | | |
| Lui dare | | | | |
| Voi stare | | | | |
| Lei capire | | | | |
| Loro finire | | | | |
| Io rispondere | | | | |
| Lui pulire | | | | |
| Noi arrivare | | | | |
| Voi salire | | | | |
| Tu soffrire | | | | |
| Lei offire | | | | |
| Io imparare | | | | |
| Lui vedere | | | | |
| Lei cadere | | | | |
| Lui morire | | | | |

## 11. Passato Prossimo and Trapassato Prossimo

Change the infinitive into the *passato prossimo* and *trapassato prossimo*.

|  |  | Passato Prossimo | Trapassato Prossimo |
|---|---|---|---|
| 1. | Io capire | _____ | _____ |
| 2. | Tu vedere | _____ | _____ |
| 3. | Lei finire | _____ | _____ |
| 4. | Lui leggere | _____ | _____ |
| 5. | Noi ritornare | _____ | _____ |
| 6. | Voi imparare | _____ | _____ |
| 7. | Loro cenare | _____ | _____ |
| 8. | Io pranzare | _____ | _____ |
| 9. | Lei vendere | _____ | _____ |
| 10. | Lui accendere | _____ | _____ |
| 11. | Voi accettare | _____ | _____ |
| 12. | Loro spegnere | _____ | _____ |
| 13. | Io lavare | _____ | _____ |
| 14. | Noi uscire | _____ | _____ |
| 15. | Tu viaggiare | _____ | _____ |
| 16. | Lui partire | _____ | _____ |
| 17. | Lei guarire | _____ | _____ |
| 18. | Voi arrivare | _____ | _____ |
| 19. | Tu ascoltare | _____ | _____ |
| 20. | Loro saltare | _____ | _____ |
| 21. | Lui esaminare | _____ | _____ |
| 22. | Noi dividere | _____ | _____ |
| 23. | Lei stirare | _____ | _____ |

# 12. Present Conditional and Past Conditional

Change the infinitive into *present conditional* and *past conditional.*

|  | | Present Conditional | Past Conditional |
|---|---|---|---|
| 1. | Io parlare | _____ | _____ |
| 2. | Tu arrivare | _____ | _____ |
| 3. | Lui cantare | _____ | _____ |
| 4. | Lei lavare | _____ | _____ |
| 5. | Lui lavorare | _____ | _____ |
| 6. | Noi stare | _____ | _____ |
| 7. | Voi andare | _____ | _____ |
| 8. | Loro viaggiare | _____ | _____ |
| 9. | Io vedere | _____ | _____ |
| 10. | Tu potere | _____ | _____ |
| 11. | Lui leggere | _____ | _____ |
| 12. | Lei scrivere | _____ | _____ |
| 13. | Noi correre | _____ | _____ |
| 14. | Voi rispondere | _____ | _____ |
| 15. | Loro cadere | _____ | _____ |
| 16. | Io capire | _____ | _____ |
| 17. | Tu finire | _____ | _____ |
| 18. | Lui venire | _____ | _____ |
| 19. | Noi sentire | _____ | _____ |
| 20. | Voi offrire | _____ | _____ |
| 21. | Loro pulire | _____ | _____ |

## 13. Subjunctive Forms

Change the infinitive into the *four* different *tenses* of the *subjunctive* as indicated.

| | Present | Imperfect | Past | Pluperfect |
|---|---|---|---|---|
| Io andare | | | | |
| Tu ritornare | | | | |
| Lui dare | | | | |
| Lei fare | | | | |
| Noi stare | | | | |
| Voi bere | | | | |
| Loro vedere | | | | |
| Noi fermare | | | | |
| Lui sentire | | | | |
| Lei dividere | | | | |
| Lui pagare | | | | |
| Tu vendere | | | | |
| Io dormire | | | | |
| Loro contare | | | | |
| Voi dire | | | | |
| Lei giocare | | | | |
| Lui saltare | | | | |
| Noi guardare | | | | |
| Tu salire | | | | |
| Voi leggere | | | | |
| Loro tirare | | | | |
| Noi pensare | | | | |

# Chapter 11

## Idiomatic Expressions with *Avere* and *Fare*

### 1. Idioms with the Verb *Avere*

Here are some common idioms with *avere.*

**Note:** The infinitive *avere* is frequently abbreviated to *aver* before a consonant. This usage is followed in the idioms presented below.

| | | |
|---|---|---|
| 1. | **avere (aver) . . . anni** | to be . . . years old |
| 2. | **aver bisogno (di)** | to need |
| 3. | **aver caldo** | to feel (be) warm |
| 4. | **aver fame** | to be hungry |
| 5. | **aver freddo** | to be cold |
| 6. | **aver fretta** | to be in a hurry |
| 7. | **avere l'impressione (di)** | to have the impression |
| 8. | **avere intenzione (di)** | to have the intention |
| 9. | **aver mal (di)** | to have an ache |
| 10. | **aver paura (di)** | to be afraid |
| 11. | **aver ragione (di)** | to be right |
| 12. | **aver sete** | to be thirsty |
| 13. | **aver sonno** | to be sleepy |
| 14. | **aver torto (di)** | to be wrong |
| 15. | **aver vergogna (di)** | to be ashamed (of) |
| 16. | **aver voglia (di)** | to feel like doing |

## 2. Practice

Rewrite in Italian, using idiomatic expressions with *avere.*

1.  I need shoes                    _____
2.  I am warm                      _____
3.  You are cold                   _____
4.  We are in a hurry              _____
5.  They have a headache           _____
6.  I am afraid                    _____
7.  She is thirsty                 _____
8.  He was sleepy                  _____
9.  They were right                _____
10. I was wrong                    _____
11. We are ashamed                 _____
12. I feel like eating             _____
13. You (pl.) were hungry          _____
14. They were in a hurry           _____
15. I would be thirsty             _____
16. They would need shoes          _____
17. She would be right             _____
18. We would be wrong              _____
19. I would be afraid              _____
20. He would have the intention    _____
21. I have had a headache          _____
22. They have been afraid          _____
23. We have been afraid            _____

## 3. Idioms with the Verb *Fare*

The verb *fare* is used in many idiomatic expressions.

**Note:** The infinitive of *fare* is frequently abbreviated to *far* before a consonant.

|     |                            |                                |
| --- | -------------------------- | ------------------------------ |
| 1.  | **fare alla romana**       | to go Dutch                    |
| 2.  | **fare bella, brutta figura** | to make a good, bad impression |
| 3.  | **fare attenzione**        | to pay attention               |
| 4.  | **fare benzina**           | to get gas                     |
| 5.  | **fa caldo, freddo**       | it is warm, cold               |
| 6.  | **fare carriera**          | to be successful               |
| 7.  | **fare colazione**         | to have breakfast              |
| 8.  | **fare colpo su qualcuno** | to impress someone             |
| 9.  | **fare compere**           | to go shopping                 |
| 10. | **fare esercizio**         | to exercise                    |
| 11. | **fare fotografie**        | to take pictures               |
| 12. | **fare il bagno**          | to take a bath                 |
| 13. | **fare la conoscenza di**  | to make the acquaintance       |
| 14. | **fare una crociera**      | to take a cruise               |
| 15. | **fare la doccia**         | to take a shower               |
| 16. | **fare lo jogging**        | to jog                         |
| 17. | **fare il pieno**          | to fill up with gas            |
| 18. | **fare la spesa**          | to get groceries               |
| 19. | **fare male**              | to hurt, to ache               |
| 20. | **fare parte di**          | to be part of                  |
| 21. | **fare una passeggiata**   | to take a walk                 |
| 22. | **fare presto**            | to hurry up                    |
| 23. | **fare progresso**         | to progress                    |

| | | |
|---|---|---|
| 24. | **fare quattro chiacchiere** | to chat |
| 25. | **fare il campeggio** | to go camping |
| 26. | **fare un complimento** | to pay a compliment |
| 27. | **fare un discorso** | to make a speech |
| 28. | **fare la predica** | to preach |
| 29. | **fare una domanda** | to ask a question |
| 30. | **fare un giro** | to take a tour |
| 31. | **fare uno spuntino** | to have a snack |
| 32. | **fare un viaggio** | to take a trip |
| 33. | **fare un regalo** | to give a gift |
| 34. | **fare visita** | to pay a visit |
| 35. | **farsi male** | to get hurt |
| 36. | **fare un favore (a)** | to do a favor |
| 37. | **fare un piacere (a)** | to do a favor |
| 38. | **far vedere a qualcuno** | to show someone |

## Weather Expressions

| | |
|---|---|
| **Che tempo fa?** | How is the weather? |
| **Fa bel tempo (cattivo).** | The weather is good (bad). |
| **Fa caldo (freddo).** | It is warm (cold). |

## 4. Practice

Rewrite in Italian, using idiomatic expressions with *fare*.

1. We go Dutch _____

2. He pays attention _____

3. I have breakfast _____

4. We take a bath _____

5. They have taken a cruise _____

6. She goes shopping _____

7. You (s.) got hurt _____

8. I do a favor _____

9. They take a walk _____

10. I'll take pictures _____

11. She took a trip _____

12. You (pl.) ask a question _____

13. He has a snack _____

14. We hurry up _____

15. It is warm _____

16. We give a gift _____

17. I pay a visit _____

18. It was cold _____

19. He preaches _____

20. She'll make a speech _____

21. They chat _____

22. He made a bad impression _____

# Verbs and Expressions Followed by Prepositions

## 5. Verbs and Expressions Followed by the Preposition *a*

### A. Before a Noun or Pronoun

| | | | |
|---|---|---|---|
| **assistere a** | to attend | **fare vedere a** | to show |
| **assomigliare a** | to resemble | **fare visita a** | to visit |
| **credere a** | to believe in | **fare un regalo a** | to give a present to |
| **dare noia a** | to bother | **giocare a** | to play a game |
| **dar da mangiare a** | to feed | **interessarsi a** | to be interested in |
| **dare fastidio a** | to bother | **partecipare a** | to participate in |
| **dare retta a** | to listen to | **pensare a** | to think about |
| **dare torto a** | to blame | **raccomandarsi a** | to ask favors of |
| **dare la caccia a** | to chase | **ricordare a** | to remind |
| **dare un calcio a** | to kick | **rinunciare a** | to give up |
| **dare un pugno a** | to punch | **servire a** | to be good for |
| **fare attenzione a** | to pay attention | **stringere la mano a** | to shake hands with |
| **fare bene (male)** | to be good (bad) | **tenere a** | to care about |
| **fare piacere a** | to please | | |

## B. Before an Infinitive

| | | | |
|---|---|---|---|
| **abituarsi a** | to get used to | **insegnare a** | to teach |
| **affrettarsi a** | to hurry | **invitare a** | to invite to |
| **aiutare a** | to help | **mandare a** | to send |
| **cominciare a** | to begin | **obbligare a** | to oblige |
| **continuare a** | to continue | **pensare a** | to think about |
| **convincere a** | to convince | **persuadere a** | to convince |
| **costringere a** | to compel | **preparare a** | to prepare |
| **decidersi a** | to make up | **provare a** | to try one's mind |
| **divertirsi a** | to have a good time | **rinunciare a** | to give up |
| **fare meglio a** | to be better off | **riprendere a** | to resume |
| **fare presto a** | to do fast | **riuscire a** | to succeed |
| **imparare a** | to learn | **sbrigarsi a** | to hurry |
| **incoraggiare a** | to encourage | **servire a** | to be good for |

## a + verbs of movement:

| | |
|---|---|
| **andare a** | to go |
| **correre a** | to run |
| **fermarsi a** | to stop |
| **passare a** | to stop by |
| **stare a** | to stay |
| **tornare a** | to return |
| **venire a** | to come |

## 6. Verbs and Expressions Followed by the Preposition *di*

### A. Before a Noun or Pronoun

| | | | |
|---|---|---|---|
| **accorgersi di** | to notice, realize | **nutrirsi di** | to feed on |
| **avere bisogno di** | to need | **occuparsi di** | to plan |
| **avere paura di** | to be afraid | **pensare di** | to have an opinion about |
| **dimenticarsi di** | to forget | **preoccuparsi di** | to worry about |
| **fidarsi di** | to trust | **ricordarsi di** | to remember |
| **innamorarsi di** | to fall in love | **ridere di** | to laugh at |
| **interessarsi di** | to be interested in | **soffrire di** | to suffer from |
| **lamentarsi di** | to complain | **trattare di** | to deal with |
| **meravigliarsi di** | to be surprised | **vivere di** | to live on |

### B. Before an Infinitive

| | | | |
|---|---|---|---|
| **accettare di** | to accept | **finire di** | to finish |
| **ammettere di** | to admit | **ordinare di** | to order |
| **aspettare di** | to wait for | **pensare di** | to plan |
| **augurare di** | to wish | **permettere di** | to permit |
| **avere bisogno di** | to need | **pregare di** | to beg |
| **cercare di** | to try | **proibire di** | to prohibit |
| **chiedere di** | to ask | **promettere di** | to promise |
| **confessare di** | to confess | **proporre di** | to propose |
| **consigliare di** | to advise | **ringraziare di** | to thank |
| **contare di** | to plan | **sapere di** | to know |
| **credere di** | to believe | **smettere di** | to stop |
| **decidere di** | to decide | **sperare di** | to hope |
| **dimenticare di** | to forget | **suggerire di** | to suggest |
| **dubitare di** | to doubt | **tentare di** | to attempt |
| **fingere di** | to pretend | **vietare di** | to avoid |

## 7. Verbs Followed by the Preposition *Su*

| | | | |
|---|---|---|---|
| **contare su** | to count on | **riflettere su** | to ponder on |
| **giurare su** | to swear on | **scommettere su** | to bet on |

## 8. Verbs Followed Directly by the Infinitive

| | | | |
|---|---|---|---|
| **amare** | to love | **piacere** | to like |
| **desiderare** | to wish | **potere** | to be able |
| **dovere** | to have to, must | **preferire** | to prefer |
| **fare** | to make | **sapere** | to know how |
| **gradire** | to appreciate | **volere** | to want |
| **lasciare** | to let, allow | | |

## 9. Impersonal Verbs

| | | | |
|---|---|---|---|
| **basta** | it is enough | **pare** | it seems |
| **bisogna** | it is necessary | | |

**Note:** These verbs may be followed directly by an infinitive.

## 10. Practice

Rewrite in English.

1. Impariamo a sciare _____

2. Comincio a capire _____

3. Ho dimenticato di studiare _____

4. Penso di venire _____

5. Ha bisogno di studiare _____

6. Pensava a te _____

7. Staremo a casa _____

8. Torneranno a Roma _____

9. Ho paura di tutto _____

10. Aspettano di venire _____

11. Ho bisogno di te _____

12. Lei continua a mangiare _____

13. Insegnava a guidare _____

14. Sperate di vedere _____

15. Mi accorgo di essere in ritardo _____

16. Si innamora di tutti _____

17. Non mi fido di lui _____

18. Lei vive di amore _____

19. Smetti di parlare! _____

20. Contate su vostra sorella _____

21. Ha tentato di camminare _____

22. Finge di guardare nel libro _____

23. Ridiamo di lui _____

24. Ringraziano di tutto _____

# 11. Practice

Rewrite in Italian.

1. I go dancing _____

2. We go study _____

3. Have you (s.) been to Rome? _____

4. I believe in ghosts _____

5. They think about vacation _____

6. I will try to come _____

7. We are thinking of going _____

8. I'll teach you to swim _____

9. I finish working _____

10. She feels like eating chocolate _____

11. I begin to speak _____

12. He stops in Paris _____

13. We try to come _____

14. Call me before you leave _____

15. You (s.) continue to study _____

16. They promised to go _____

17. I promised to come _____

18. They need to think _____

19. You (pl.) hope to sleep _____

20. They feel like traveling _____

21. Stop (s.) talking! _____

22. They pay attention to the teacher _____

# Chapter 12

## Final Review of Verbs

This extra opportunity for review will reinforce your command of the kinds of conjugations you have learned throughout the book, while giving you the chance to use verbs in complete sentences. For each of the exercises, rewrite the sentence(s) in Italian with the correct tense of the verb indicated.

### -are Verbs

**abitare:** to live, to inhabit, to occupy

1. Where do you live? I live in Naples. _____

2. They have lived in Italy for a long time. _____

3. When I was young I lived in Florida. _____

4. He would like to live in a big house. _____

5. She hopes to live near the sea. _____


**addormentare:** to put to sleep, to sleep, to be boring, to make sleepy

6. This movie puts me to sleep. _____

7. It is a boring book. _____

8. This lesson makes me sleepy. _____

9. I fall asleep with the light on. _____


**addormentarsi:** to fall asleep, to go to sleep

10. Paul falls asleep in front of the television. _____

11. Don't fall asleep at the movie. _____

12. The child fell asleep right away. _____


**alzare (qualche cosa):** to lift, to raise, to build

13. Please raise the heat; I am cold. _____

14. He should raise his voice; nobody can hear him. _____

**alzarsi:** to get up, to rise, to get tall

15. The young man gets up late all the time. _____

16. The sun rises late in winter. _____


**andare:** to go, to drive, to fly, to have to, to be needed

17. They go to school at eight o'clock. _____

18. Where did you go last night? _____

19. I would like her to go to college. _____

20. She drove to Rome with me. _____

21. In March we'll fly to Italy. _____


**andare a:** to go to

22. I am not going to school this evening. _____

23. Would you like to go dancing? _____

24. Next month I will go to visit some friends. _____

25. Could you go to the post office? _____

26. Next week I will go to the museum. _____

27. She would like to go skiing with us. _____


**andare da + article:** to go to

28. She went to the doctor. _____

29. I would like to go to the butcher. _____

30. I think they went to their friend. _____


**andare in:** to go to, to go in, to go by

31. Next year I would like to go to Italy. _____

32. She will go to China with some friends. _____

33. Will they go by car or by plane? _____

34. My mom went in the kitchen. _____

**arrivare:** to arrive

35. My friends will arrive tomorrow. _____

36. Your ticket arrived yesterday. _____

37. I hope they arrived well. _____


**arrivare a:** to arrive at (place or city)

38. They have arrived at the airport. _____

39. I will arrive in Venice in a week. _____


**arrivare in:** to arrive (country singular), means of transportation

40. They arrived in America by boat. _____

41. She said she has arrived in China. _____

42. I would like to arrive in Greece in summer. _____

43. I will arrive tomorrow by car. _____


**arrivare in:** to arrive in (country plural)

44. We arrived in the United States. _____

45. The tourists arrive in summer. _____


**aspettare:** to wait for

46. I am waiting for my sister. _____

47. I waited for him for a long time. _____


**chiamare:** to call, to call for, to send for

48. They called a cab an hour ago. _____

49. She is very ill; we must call a doctor. _____

50. They want to phone her, but it is too late. _____

**chiamarsi:** to be named, to call oneself

51. I don't know what your name is. _____

52. What is your sister's name? Her name is Carla. _____


**dare:** to give, to pay, to set, to award, to give off, to show, to lend, to take

53. I gave him a book. _____

54. She hoped they would award him the first prize. _____

55. Could you lend me your car on Saturday? _____

56. The president handed in his resignation. _____

57. She gave me a lot of money. _____


**desiderare:** to wish for, to want, to need, would like

58. The boy wishes for many gifts at Christmas. _____

59. Carlo wants to talk to you. _____

60. Is there anything you need to see? _____

61. At the restaurant she wanted to taste everything. _____

62. Would you like a cup of coffee or tea? _____

63. We want you to come to visit us. _____


**diventare:** to become, to get, to grow, to make

64. Carla has grown very tall. _____

65. Verdi became very famous. _____

66. People in Italy are getting very old. _____

67. She has become a beautiful girl. _____


**fare:** to do, to make, to have, to cook, to bake, to walk, to perform

68. What do you suggest that I do? _____

69. She bakes cookies every day. _____

70. She made a beautiful dress. _____

71. I would like to be a teacher. _____

72. Yesterday it was very cold. _____

73. In summer it is very hot. _____

74. I hope you will have a nice vacation. _____

75. They are building a new road. _____

76. He hoped to go for a long walk. _____

77. The artist made a beautiful statue. _____


**guardare:** to look at/down/forward/after, to watch, to stare, to guard

78. The teacher looks at him. _____

79. Did you look over her homework? _____

80. He was staring at me. _____


**mandare:** to send

81. She sends the children to bed. _____

82. She sent the children to bed. _____

83. I will send the package right away. _____

84. I hoped you would send me your book. _____

85. You must send the book by mail. _____

86. I am sending you a kiss. _____


**pensare:** to think, to imagine, to guess

87. I think it is too cold to go out. _____

88. Guess who I saw last night? _____

89. They should have thought about it. _____


**sognare:** to dream, to imagine

90. I dreamed I was flying. _____

91. Giovanna was daydreaming. _____

92. I would have never imagined winning the lottery. _____

**stare:** to stay, to be, to be located, to live

93. The children want to stay inside today. _____

94. I will stay in Italy for two weeks._____

95. Kids, be quiet. _____

96. My mother was at the window. _____

97. My friends live in Rome. _____

## -ere Verbs

**accendere:** to light, to turn on

1. Turn on the light, please. _____

2. I do not want you to light a cigarette._____

**avere:** to have, to feel, to wear

3. Her son has the flu. _____

4. Their relatives do not have any money to live._____

5. I would have done it, if I had had time. _____

6. They used to have many friends. _____

7. Are you hungry? Yes, I am very hungry._____

8. That boy is very lucky._____

9. My girlfriend is always in a hurry._____

10. The lady was wearing a beautiful dress. _____

**bere:** to drink

11. That man drinks too much. _____

12. Let us drink to our health. _____

13. I think he likes to drink red wine. _____

**chiedere:** to ask for, to charge, to take

14. She asked me for help._____

15. My mother always asks about you. _____

16. How much do you charge for this house? _____

**chiudere:** to close, to shut, to turn off

17. The shops close at 7:30. _____

18. You never shut the door. _____

19. Did you close the bottle? _____

20. She shut him out of the house. _____


**conoscere:** to know, to be familiar, to meet

21. Your father knows Italy well. _____

22. Do you know a good doctor? _____

23. I met my husband in Africa. _____

24. I did not know her very well. _____


**correre:** to run, to go fast, to rush

25. That boy was running like the wind. _____

26. The train runs fast. _____

27. We must run to get the bus. _____

28. Kids cannot run at the pool. _____


**credere a, in:** to believe in

29. Nobody believes him. _____

30. Paul does not believe in God. _____


**credere che:** to believe, to think that

31. I did not believe they had already arrived. _____

32. He believes it will rain tomorrow. _____


**decidere di:** to decide, to resolve to

33. I cannot decide when to go to Italy. _____

34. He decided to respect the rules. _____

35. They will decide soon where to go on vacation. _____

**difendere:** to defend, to plead, to protect

36. She always defends her brother. _____

37. The soldiers defended the town. _____

38. The gloves protect your hands from the cold. _____


**dispiacere:** to regret, to mind

39. Would you mind if I came home with you? _____

40. I regret not being able to visit you. _____

41. If you don't mind, I would like to rest. _____

42. I am sorry that your mother could not come. _____


**dovere:** must, to need to, ought to, to have to

43. What should I do? _____

44. I should not tell you this story. _____

45. Carlo was to become a great writer. _____

46. You do not need to buy it today. _____


**essere:** to be, to exist, to happen

47. Where are you from? Are you American? _____

48. What time is it? Is it early, or is it late? _____

49. Paolo is not at home. _____

50. What will be, will be. _____

51. It is not possible that they will come. _____

52. It was not possible for them to come. _____

53. What happened? _____


**mettere:** to put, to place, to stick, to hang

54. We put all the books on the desk. _____

55. We have hung the curtains. _____

56. Have you put away the suitcases? _____

**mettersi:** to place, to put on oneself

57. She put on her new bathing suit. _____

58. She started to cry. _____

59. He placed himself near the window. _____

**nascere:** to be born, to rise, to sprout

60. My son was born on October 12. _____

61. Do you think that I was born yesterday? _____

62. Your sister was born in Venice. _____

63. The sun rises in the East. _____

64. They sprout like mushrooms. _____

**rispondere:** to answer, to reply, to respond

65. I hope you will answer my letter. _____

66. Why didn't you answer my question? _____

67. Nobody answers the phone. _____

**rispondere di:** to be responsible for, to vouch for

68. The kids have to pay for the broken glass. _____

69. She is responsible for his actions. _____

**scrivere:** to write, to spell, to say

70. How is your last name spelled? _____

71. Should I type the letter? _____

72. She has written to the Italian consulate. _____

73. Dante wrote a lot in his life. _____

74. She hopes you will write her soon. _____

75. I wrote him not to come. _____

**tenere:** to keep, to hold, to hold on to, to hold back, to have, to occupy

76. The little boy was holding a toy in his hand. _____

77. The police were holding the people back. _____

78. I kept the water in the refrigerator. _____

79. May I keep my coat on? I am cold. _____

80. She wants to keep the windows closed. _____


**vedere:** to see, to show

81. Have you seen a good movie? _____

82. I would like to see him happy. _____

83. I cannot wait to leave for Italy. _____

84. Does the stain still show? _____

85. We saw a star falling. _____

86. He will go to see his mother. _____

87. They used to go to see him ski. _____


**vendere:** to sell

88. He sells books. _____

89. She has sold many houses. _____

90. They sell wholesale. _____

91. I do not like to sell. _____


**volere:** to want to, to refuse to, to mean to

92. They would like to travel, but they cannot. _____

93. Today my car refuses to work. _____

94. She does not want you to come tomorrow. _____

95. I wish you would tell her. _____

96. She wants to study Italian. _____

97. We want to see your paintings. _____

98. He wants to buy a new car. _____

## -*ire* Verbs

**aprire:** to open, to start, to turn on

1. Open the door, please. _____

2. He wants to open a checking account. _____

3. Do not turn on the television._____

4. The band was leading the parade. _____


**aprirsi:** to open, to bloom

5. The spring flowers have bloomed. _____

6. The windows in the apartment open to the sea._____

7. School opens in the fall._____


**costruire:** to build, to construct

8. They are building a new highway. _____

9. I hope to build a new house._____

10. With hard work, you can build a fortune. _____


**dire:** to say, to tell, to speak, to express

11. Young children often tell lies._____

12. His father told him so. _____

13. She told them to call us when they arrive. _____

14. I hope you did not say anything._____

15. Tell him the truth! _____

16. The witness declared that he had not seen the accident. _____


**divertire:** to amuse, to entertain

17. Cartoons entertain children._____

18. The lady has fun with the children. _____

**divertirsi:** to enjoy oneself, to have fun

19. Did you enjoy yourself in New York? _____

20. Have fun! _____

21. That child has fun playing with Legos. _____

22. I do not have fun at the circus. _____


**finire:** to end, to finish, to be done, to stop

23. I already know how the book ends. _____

24. The lesson ends at 9:00 P.M. _____

25. Are you done? _____

26. Did you spend all the money? _____

27. The ice cream is all gone. _____

28. I did not finish my homework. _____


**partire:** to depart, to leave, to take off

29. They departed by plane for Italy. _____

30. My friends left yesterday for the beach. _____

31. The train takes off at exactly 10:00 A.M. _____

32. I will leave on Tuesday. _____

33. They left early. _____


**preferire:** to prefer, to like better

34. My mother likes coffee better than tea. _____

35. I would rather read than watch television. _____

36. I prefer that you stay inside. _____

37. They prefer downhill skiing to skating. _____


**pulire:** to clean

38. Every Friday I clean my house. _____

39. Clean your shoes before you come in. _____

40. Clean your nose. _____

**salire:** to go, to come up, to climb, to ascend, to rise

41. The spacecraft was rising very fast. _____

42. You have to come up to the third floor. _____

43. The price of fruit has gone up again. _____

44. She has to get on the bus. _____

45. My daughter went up with the elevator. _____

**sentire:** to hear, to listen, to know

46. The mother heard the baby cry. _____

47. Did you listen to the concert? _____

48. I would like to know your opinion. _____

49. My grandfather does not hear well. _____

**soffrire:** to suffer, to stand, to bear

50. Giovanna has been suffering from a headache. _____

51. They suffered from hunger. _____

52. The orange trees have suffered from the frost. _____

**spedire:** to mail, to ship

53. I will mail you a letter. _____

54. They shipped you a big box. _____

55. I would like to mail you a gift. _____

**uscire:** to leave, to go out, to get out, to lead

56. Your father went out on foot. _____

57. My friends left half an hour ago. _____

58. Do not go out. It is raining. _____

**venire:** to come

59. Would you like to come with us? _____

60. They came to Italy many years ago. _____

61. I think someone is coming. _____

62. At what time did you come home? _____

63. Where does that girl come from? _____

64. This oil comes from the farm. _____

65. The snow was coming down slowly. _____

# Answer Key

## Chapter 1

### Page 5, Practice 8

1. canto, canti, canta, cantiamo, cantate, cantano
2. provo, provi, prova, proviamo, provate, provano
3. lavoro, lavori, lavora, lavoriamo, lavorate, lavorano
4. ricordo, ricordi, ricorda, ricordiamo, ricordate, ricordano
5. viaggio, viaggi, viaggia, viaggiamo, viaggiate, viaggiano
6. volo, voli, vola, voliamo, volate, volano

### Page 6, Practice 9

| | |
|---|---|
| Io: | studio, insegno, viaggio, salto |
| Tu: | parli, mangi, trovi, balli |
| Lui, Lei: | impara, entra, lava, riposa |
| Noi: | compriamo, arriviamo, aiutiamo, tagliamo |
| Voi: | parlate, imparate, aspettate, pensate |
| Loro: | spiegano, insegnano, contano, camminano |

### Page 7, Practice 10

1. mangiamo, 2. impara, 3. comprano, 4. canto, 5. cammini, 6. parlate, 7. studiamo, 8. cambia, 9. pensate, 10. nuota, 11. gioco, 12. pranziamo, 13. viaggiate, 14. ballano, 15. lavora, 16. laviamo, 17. penso, 18. impariamo, 19. ascolto, 20. ama, 21. abitate, 22. pagano, 23. entri, 24. ispezioniamo, 25. pensa, 26. mandi

### Page 8, Practice 11

1. we eat, 2. I learn, 3. they buy, 4. I sing, 5. you (s.) walk, 6. you (pl.) speak, 7. we study, 8. I change, 9. you (pl.) think, 10. I swim, 11. I play, 12. we have lunch, 13. you (pl.) travel, 14. they dance, 15. he/she works, 16. we wash, 17. I think, 18. we learn, 19. I listen, 20. he/she loves, 21. you (pl.) live, 22. they pay, 23. you (s.) enter, 24. we inspect, 25. he/she thinks, 26. you (s.) send

### Page 9, Practice 12

1. mangio, 2. pensi, 3. imparano, 4. cantiamo, 5. mangiate, 6. lui studia, 7. lei insegna, 8. imparo, 9. lavori, 10. lavano, 11. lei entra, 12. riposiamo, 13. aspetti, 14. cantano, 15. ballo, 16. saltiamo, 17. viaggio, 18. lui trova, 19. arriviamo, 20. aspettate, 21. lei aiuta, 22. compro, 23. lei trova, 24. studiamo

#### Negative and Interrogative Forms

1. non mangio, 2. non lavori, 3. non ricordiamo, 4. non lavorano, 5. non entra, 6. io non riposo, 7 mangi?, 8. lavori?, 9. ricordiamo?, 10. lavorano?, 11. entra?, 12. riposo?

### Page 10, Practice 13

1. we speak, 2. you (s.) jump, 3. he/she thinks, 4. you (pl.) sing, 5. I play, 6. we eat, 7. they learn, 8. you (s.) find, 9. we enter, 10. you (s.) work, 11. we teach, 12. you (pl.) wash, 13. I rest, 14. he/she looks, 15. we walk, 16. you (pl.) bring, 17. you (s.) dance, 18. they speak, 19. he/she travels, 20. we help, 21. I remember, 22. he/she forgets, 23. I don't eat, 24. they don't walk, 25. you (pl.) don't work, 26. do you (s.) work?

### Page 12, Practice 15

1. do, dai, dà, diamo, date, danno
2. faccio, fai, fa, facciamo, fate, fanno
3. sto, stai, sta, stiamo, state, stanno
4. vado, vai, va, andiamo, andate, vanno

# Chapter 2

### Page 15, Practice 3

1. divido, dividi, divide, dividiamo, dividete, dividono
2. chiudo, chiudi, chiude, chiudiamo, chiudete, chiudono
3. metto, metti, mette, mettiamo, mettete, mettono
4. convinco, convinci, convince, convinciamo, convincete, convincono
5. spingo, spingi, spinge, spingiamo, spingete, spingono
6. perdo, perdi, perde, perdiamo, perdete, perdono

### Page 16, Practice 4

| | |
|---|---|
| Io: | apprendo, attendo, chiedo, chiudo |
| Tu: | cadi, confondi, dividi, cresci |
| Lui, Lei: | decide, difende, discute, conclude |
| Noi: | apprendiamo, attendiamo, insistiamo, esistiamo |
| Voi: | cadete, ridete, rispondete, nascondete |
| Loro: | perdono, piangono, insistono, promettono |

### Page 17, Practice 5

1. temo, 2. attendi, 3. cade, 4. chiediamo, 5. assisti, 6. chiude, 7. confondono, 8. conosci, 9. decidono, 10. difende, 11. discute, 12. decidiamo, 13. chiede, 14. godi, 15. concludo, 16. insiste, 17. mettiamo, 18. perde, 19. prometto, 20. promettiamo, 21. piangiamo, 22. rispondono, 23. vedo, 24. vede, 25. scrivo, 26. piango

**Negative and Interrogative Forms**

1. non assisto, 2. non attendi, 3. non chiediamo, 4. non dividono, 5. non chiude, 6. non piange, 7. assisti?, 8. attendi?, 9. chiedi?, 10. dividono?, 11. chiudi?, 12. piangi?

### Page 18, Practice 6

1. we learn, 2. he/she fears, 3. we assume, 4. they attend, 5. I fall, 6. you (pl.) believe, 7. he/she asks, 8. they close, 9. you (s.) correct, 10. you (pl.) conclude, 11. they share, 12. they confuse, 13. you (s.) know, 14. they know, 15. you (pl.) cook, 16. he/she cooks, 17. I decide, 18. you (pl.) defend, 19. we discuss, 20. we include, 21. he/she insists, 22. you (pl.) lose, 23. they lose, 24. they cry, 25. he/she pretends, 26. you (s.) answer, 27. I see, 28. you (s.) win, 29. he/she knows, 30. they win, 31. you (pl.) laugh, 32. they break, 33. I don't stay, 34. they don't allow, 35. we don't read, 36. do you (pl.) read?, 37. do you (s.) read?, 38. do we see?, 39. does he/she write?, 40. do they fear?, 41. don't you (pl.) see?, 42. don't you (s.) read?, 43. don't they write?, 44. don't we write?

### Page 20, Practice 8

1. devo, devi, deve, dobbiamo, dovete, devono
2. scelgo, scegli, sceglie, scegliamo, scegliete, scelgono
3. posso, puoi, può, possiamo, potente, possono
4. so, sai, sa, sappiamo, sapete, sanno
5. tengo, tieni, tiene, teniamo, tenete, tengono
6. voglio, vuoi, vogliamo, volete, vogliono

### Page 23, Practice 10

1. avverto, avverti, avverte, avvertiamo, avvertite, avvertono
2. bollo, bolli, bolle, bolliamo, bollite, bollono
3. sento, senti, sente, sentiamo, sentite, sentono
4. capisco, capisci, capisce, capiamo, capite, capiscono
5. preferisco, preferisci, preferisce, preferiamo, preferite, preferiscono

| Io: | apro, capisco, offro, finisco |
| Tu: | dormi, avverti, bolli, senti |
| Lui, Lei: | preferisce, parte, veste, spedisce |
| Noi: | serviamo, vestiamo, apriamo, capiamo |
| Voi: | avvertite, seguite, costruite, istruite |
| Loro: | sentono, inseguono, investono, partono |

**Page 25, Practice 12**

1. preferisco, 2. acconsenti, 3. copre, 4. godiamo, 5. fuggono, 6. capisce, 7. segue, 8. menti, 9. sento, 10. soffriamo, 11. aprono, 12. finisce, 13. applaudi, 14. converte, 15. applaudo, 16. dorme, 17. inghiottisco, 18. partite, 19. servono, 20. dormo, 21. preferisce, 22. capisco, 23. preferiamo, 24. costruisco

**Negative and Interrogative Forms**

1. non finisco, 2. non capisce, 3. non istruiscono, 4. non senti, 5. non dormo, 6. non applaudiamo, 7. non partiamo, 8. non soffro, 9. costruiamo?, 10. sente?, 11. capiscono?, 12. sentono?, 13. dorme?, 14. acconsenti?, 15. finisce?, 16. partiamo?

**Page 26, Practice 13**

1. you (s.) agree, 2. they applaud, 3. he/she opens, 4. they open, 5. we announce, 6. he/she boils, 7. I understand, 8. you (pl.) consent, 9. they convert, 10. I cover, 11. he/she builds, 12. he/she offers, 13. we enjoy, 14. you (pl.) sleep, 15. they follow, 16. we finish, 17. he/she escapes, 18. you (s.) heal, 19. they guarantee, 20. you (s.) swallow, 21. they chase, 22. he/she instructs, 23. they prefer, 24. you (pl.) follow, 25. you (pl.) clean, 26. they punish, 27. he/she hits, 28. I serve, 29. he/she suffers, 30. I substitute, 31. we send, 32. they substitute, 33. we suggest, 34. they transfer

**Negative and Interrogative Forms**

1. we don't sleep, 2. he/she doesn't suffer, 3. we don't understand, 4. he/she doesn't instruct, 5. you (s.) don't open, 6. do you (s.) agree?, 7. do they leave?, 8. do you (s.) sleep?, 9. do you (s.) understand?, 10. do you (pl.) clean?

**Page 28, Practice 15**

1. vengo, vieni, viene, veniamo, venite, vengono
2. dico, dici, dice. diciamo, dite, dicono
3. esco, esci, esce, usciamo, uscite, escono

**Page 28, Practice 16**

1. dici, 2. escono, 3. veniamo, 4. muoiono, 5. salto, 6. dice, 7. esco, 8. vengono, 9. salgono, 10. usciamo, 11. salite, 12. muore, 13. odi, 14. dicono, 15. udiamo, 16. dite

# Chapter 3

**Page 30, Practice 3**

1. parla, 2. canta, 3. andate, 4. non andare, 5. andiamo, 6. non mangiate, 7. finiamo, 8. non giocate, 9. gioca, 10. guarda, 11. ascolta, 12. non partire, 13. partiamo, 14. giocate, 15. giochiamo, 16. esci, 17. non uscite, 18. gioca, 19. non giocare, 20. mangiate, 21. scrivi, 22. non scrivere, 23. scriviamo, 24. chiudi, 25. non chiudere, 26. chiudiamo, 27. dormi, 28. dormite, 29. bevi, 30. bevete, 31. leggi, 32. leggiamo, 33. non leggere, 34. non leggete

**Page 31, Practice 4**

1. speak (pl.), 2. sing, 3. don't sing, 4. listen, 5. listen (pl.), 6. let's go, 7. speak, 8. don't speak, 9. let's play, 10. don't play (pl.), 11. go out (pl.), 12. don't go out, 13. eat, 14. let's eat, 15. close, 16. ask (pl.), 17. think, 18. don't think (pl.), 19. suggest, 20. leave, 21. put (pl.), 22. don't put, 23. hope, 24. come in (pl.), 25. study, 26. don't study, 27. don't leave (pl.), 28. sing, 29. let's sing, 30. push, 31. don't push, 32. take (pl.)

**Page 33, Practice 7**

1. aspetti, 2. aspettino, 3. paghi, 4. paghino, 5. mangi, 6. rispondano, 7. finisca, 8. guardino, 9. venga, 10. mangino, 11. risponda, 12. finiscano, 13. vengano, 14. esca, 15. partino, 16. mi dica, 17. pensi, 18. escano, 19. cammini, 20. cantino, 21. leggano, 22. sorrida

**Page 35, Practice 9**

1. vedrò, vedrai, vedrà, vedremo, vedrete, vedranno
2. andrò, andrai, andrà, andremo, andrete, andranno
3. capirò, capirai, capirà, capiremo, capirete, capiranno
4. aiuterò, aiuterai, aiuterà, aiuteremo, aiuterete, aiuteranno

**Page 36, Practice 10**

| | |
|---|---|
| Io: | parlerò, vedrò, pulirò |
| Tu: | viaggerai, permetterai, capirai |
| Lui, Lei: | troverà, saprà, sentirà |
| Noi: | guarderemo, berremo, finiremo |
| Voi: | lavorerete, avrete, partirete |
| Loro: | andranno, saranno, sentiranno |

**Page 37, Practice 11**

1. I'll understand, 2. I'll work, 3. you'll (s.) read, 4. he/she'll sing, 5. you'll (pl.) hear, 6. you'll (s.) plant, 7. I'll listen, 8. you'll (pl.) plant, 9. we'll see, 10. they'll answer, 11. I'll pay, 12. we'll play, 13. you'll (s.) think, 14. you'll (pl.) see, 15. you'll (s.) hear, 16. I'll decide, 17. we'll cry, 18. he/she'll win, 19. you'll (pl.) discuss, 20. we'll go, 21. I'll study, 22. you'll (pl.) think, 23. you'll (s.) write, 24. I'll cook, 25. I'll finish, 26. we'll play, 27. we'll stay, 28. you'll (s.) do/make, 29. you'll (pl.) give, 30. you'll (s.) leave, 31. you'll (pl.) tell, 32. we'll sleep, 33. you'll (s.) chase, 34. we'll come, 35. I'll boil, 36. they'll applaud, 37. he/she'll open, 38. we'll climb
**Negative Future Forms**
1. I won't eat, 2. we won't go, 3. he/she won't do/make, 4. we won't sing, 5. he/she won't understand, 6. you (pl.) won't finish

**Page 38, Practice 12**

1. attenderò, 2. cadrà, 3. scriveremo, 4. penseranno, 5. capiremo, 6. chiuderò, 7. parlerai, 8. giocheremo, 9. viaggeranno, 10. metterò, 11. faremo, 12. troverà, 13. troveremo, 14. ascolterò, 15. impareremo, 16. mangerò, 17. andremo, 18. faranno, 19. starò, 20. comprerò, 21. verranno, 22. verrò, 23. guarderemo, 24. diremo, 25. dirà, 26. canteranno, 27. piangeremo, 28. pianterò, 29. usciremo, 30. saliranno, 31. andrete, 32. seguiremo, 33. insisterà, 34. vedrà, 35. risponderemo, 36. pagherò, 37. voteremo, 38. deciderò, 39. berremo, 40. sentiremo
**Negative Future Forms**
1. non mangerò, 2. non ascolterà, 3. non berremo, 4. non mangeranno

# Chapter 4

**Page 40, Practice 3**

1. pensavo, pensavi, pensava, pensavamo, pensavate, pensavano
2. bevevo, bevevi, beveva, bevevamo, bevevate, bevevano
3. finivo, finivi, finiva, finivamo, finivate, finivano
4. abitavo, abitavi, abitava, abitavamo, abitavate, abitavano

**Page 41, Practice 4**

| | |
|---|---|
| Io: | mangiavo, mettevo, sentivo |
| Tu: | cantavi, vedevi, finivi |
| Lui, Lei: | saltava, beveva, apriva |
| Noi: | votavamo, rispondevamo, costruivamo |
| Voi: | giocavate, comprendevate, applaudivate |
| Loro: | speravano, vendevano, preferivano |

**Page 42, Practice 5**

**A.** 1. parlava, 2. cantavate, 3. abitava, 4. partivamo, 5. giocavate, 6. finivano, 7. camminavo, 8. perdevi, 9. comprendevate, 10. mangiavano, 11. costruivi, 12. istruivate, 13. lavorava, 14. ballava, 14. pensavano, 16. credevate, 17. lavavi, 18. scrivevamo, 19. correvo, 20. parlava

**B.** **Note:** The imperfect can be translated as **used to** or **was + verb ending in ing.** 1. we used to eat, 2. you (s.) used to study, 3. you (s.) used to drink, 4. you (s.) were playing, 5. he/she was listening, 6. you (pl.) used to understand, 7. they were writing, 8. I was asking, 9. you (pl.) were closing, 10. he/she used to listen, 11. we used to take, 12. I was learning, 13. we used to sell, 14, you (s.) used to sell, 15. you (s.) used to understand, 16. they were living, 17. he/she was instructing, 18. he/she used to see, 19. they were receiving, 20. I was teaching

**Page 43, Practice 6**

1. mangiavano, 2. pensavamo, 3. venivi, 4. credevo, 5. non pensavano, 6. imparavo, 7. credevano, 8. chiedevamo, 9. non volevi, 10. aspettava, 11. imparavano, 12. capivo, 13. potevi, 14. cantavamo, 15. volevano, 16. pensavo, 17. pensavamo, 18. voleva, 19. andava, 20. aspettavo, 21. speravo, 22. speravamo, 23. parlavo, 24. studiavi?, 25. parlavi?, 26. sperava, 27. pensavi, 28. lavoravamo, 29. volevano, 30. guardavamo, 31. guardavamo?, 32. viaggiava, 33. insegnavo, 34. mangiavano, 35. non capivo, 36. non potevo, 37. cantavano, 38. non volevano, 39. non pensavo, 40. pensavi, 41. voleva, 42. pulivo, 43. guardavamo, 44. non speravano, 45. sperava, 46. dubitavi

**Page 44, Practice 9**

1. mangiai, mangiasti, mangiò, mangiammo, mangiaste, mangiarono
2. potei, potesti, potè, potemmo, poteste, poterono
3. capii, capisti, capì, capimmo, capiste, capirono

**Page 46, Practice 11**

| | |
|---|---|
| Io: | chiesi, conobbi, sentii |
| Tu: | comprasti, temesti, finisti |
| Carlo: | nacque, vide, volle |
| Maria: | capì, scrisse, venne |
| Noi: | facemmo, bevemmo, ridemmo |
| Voi: | scendeste, vinceste, metteste |
| Loro: | offrirono, partirono, fecero |

**Page 47, Practice 12**

1. I came, 2. I laughed, 3. I drank, 4. he fell, 5. she asked, 6. we closed, 7. you (pl.) knew, 8. you (s.) said, 9. she decided, 10. we said, 11. you (pl.) must, 12. they said, 13. I lived, 14. they won, 15. you (s.) did/made, 16. she read, 17. we read, 18. you (s.) put, 19. you (pl.) were born, 20. I took, 21. we took, 22. you (s.) laughed, 23. they laughed, 24. she stayed, 25. you (s.) chose, 26. they wrote, 27. I chose, 28. you (s.) chose, 29. they wrote, 30. you (pl.) stayed, 31. you (s.) saw, 32. we saw, 33. you (pl.) won, 34. I saw, 35. they saw, 36. she lived, 37. he wanted, 38. we wanted, 39. they came, 40. you (s.) stayed

**Page 48, Practice 13**

1. I speak, 2. we eat, 3. they live, 4. do you (pl.) live?, 5. we drive, 6. I don't work, 7. we'll return, 8. they'll return, 9. I don't fly, 10. do you (pl.) fly?, 11. they'll arrive, 12. I'll arrive, 13. you won't (pl.) arrive, 14. I ask, 15. I wasn't asking, 16. they close, 17. do you (s.) close?, 18. I think, 19. you'll (s.) think, 20. we rest, 21. they rest, 22. you (s.) don't rest, 23. I spoke, 24. we thought, 25. do you (s.) rest?, 26. eat!, 27. look (pl.)!, 28. speak!, 29. learn!, 30. don't look!, 31. don't sleep!, 32. listen (formal)!, 33. do you (s.) promise?, 34. I'll answer, 35. we'll write, 36. I used to read, 37. you (s.) used to speak, 38. you (pl.) wanted, 39. they used to cry, 40. you (s.) used to insist, 41. you (s.) used to drink, 42. drink!, 43. drink! (pl.), 44. don't drink!, 45. you (s.) come, 46. do you (s.) come?, 47. he/she read, 48. you (pl.) heard

**Page 49, Practice 14**

1. abitano, 2. aprivo, 3. lavorarono, 4. saliamo, 5. capisco, 6. mangiarono, 7. mangiammo, 8. lavora, 9. studiano, 10. tengo, 11. scrivo, 12. scrivevi, 13. scriverò, 14. viaggi, 15. viaggiavi, 16. viaggeranno, 17. parto, 18. parte, 19. partiremo, 20. partiva, 21. imparava, 22. imparavamo, 23. pensavano, 24. vivrò, 25. apriremo, 26. mangia!, 27. lavora!, 28. mangerà, 29. lavorerà, 30. studia!, 31. studiate!, 32. bevi!, 33. bevete!, 34. promettevamo, 35. volevo, 36. deve, 37. rispondi!, 38. scriva!, 39. aspetti!, 40. dissi, 41. aspetteremo, 42. discuto, 43. vedevamo, 44. sanno, 45. capiamo, 46. pensavo

# Chapter 5

### Page 56, Practice 7

1. ho mangiato, hai mangiato, ha mangiato, abbiamo mangiato, avete mangiato, hanno mangiato
2. ho scritto, hai scritto, ha scritto, abbiamo scritto, avete scritto, hanno scritto
3. sono venuto/a, sei venuto/a, è venuto/a, siamo venuti/e, siete venuti/e, sono venuti/e
4. sono andato/a, sei andato/a, è andato/a, siamo andati/e, siete andati/e, sono andati/e

### Page 57, Practice 8

| | | | |
|---|---|---|---|
| Io: | ho mangiato | ho visto | ho sentito |
| Tu: | hai parlato | hai scritto | hai capito |
| Lui: | ha viaggiato | ha potuto | ha finito |
| Lei: | ha camminato | ha voluto | è venuta |
| Noi: | abbiamo lodato | abbiamo spinto | siamo saliti/e |
| Voi: | siete stati/e | avete riso | avete aperto |
| Loro: | hanno dato | sono rimasti/e | hanno nutrito |
| Carlo: | ha fatto | è nato | ha offerto |
| Maria: | è andata | ha nascosto | ha pulito |
| Io e Giovanni: | abbiamo aspettato | abbiamo venduto | siamo partiti |
| Tu e Pietro: | avete imparato | avete chiuso | siete usciti |
| Giovanni e Paolo: | hanno fermato | hanno vissuto | hanno finito |

### Page 58, Practice 9

| | | | |
|---|---|---|---|
| Io: | non sono stato/a | non ho avuto | non ho potuto |
| Tu: | non hai voluto | non hai dovuto | non hai capito |
| Lui: | non ha fatto | non ha dato | non è stato |
| Noi: | non siamo andati/e | non siamo arrivati/e | non siamo partiti/e |

### Page 59, Practice 10

1. ha parlato, 2. siamo stati/e, 3. è stata, 4. avete letto, 5. hanno sentito, 6. ho dormito, 7. hai perso, 8. è andata, 9. ha deciso, 10. abbiamo comprato, 11. avete vissuto, 12. hanno bevuto, 13. ha parlato, 14. ha aperto, 15. ha aperto, 16. avete imparato, 17. abbiamo temuto, 18. ho mangiato, 19. hai ricevuto, 20. ha lavorato, 21. abbiamo viaggiato, 22. hanno potuto, 23. avete insegnato, 24. abbiamo sciato, 25. abbiamo corso, 26. ho guardato, 27. hai guarito, 28. avete risposto, 29. sono arrivati/e, 39. abbiamo tenuto, 31. ha venduto, 32. hanno vissuto, 33. ho abitato, 34. abbiamo gettato

### Page 59, Practice 11

1. non ha mangiato, 2. non ha comprato, 3. non hai parlato, 4. non ho studiato, 5. non hanno dovuto, 6. non abbiamo cantato, 7. non hanno visto, 8. non avete sentito, 9. non hai scritto, 10. non abbiamo voluto

**Page 60, Practice 12**

1. abbiamo risposto, 2. hanno comprato, 3. abbiamo imparato, 4. ha comprato, 5. ho chiesto, 6. hai risposto, 7. abbiamo lasciato, 8. ho bevuto, 9. non ho bevuto, 10. hanno insegnato, 11. ho letto, 12. hai scritto, 13. hanno lavorato, 14. ha dormito, 15. ha lavorato, 16. abbiamo studiato, 17. non ha sciato, 18. non è andata, 19. è nata, 20. hanno venduto, 21. non ho ascoltato, 22. non ho sentito, 23. non ho chiesto, 24. non hai risposto, 25. ho ricevuto, 26. ho imparato, 27. hanno capito, 28. ha viaggiato, 29. non abbiamo viaggiato, 30. hanno pulito, 31. abbiamo pensato, 32. non hanno pensato, 33. ho pulito, 34. hai pagato, 35. non hai pagato, 36. abbiamo mangiato, 37. sono arrivato/a, 38. sono stati/e

**Page 61, Practice 15**

1. avevo guardato, avevi guardato, aveva guardato, avevamo guardato, avevate guardato, avevano guardato
2. avevo visto, avevi visto, aveva visto, avevamo visto, avevate visto, avevano visto
3. ero partito/a, eri partito/a, era partito/a, eravamo partiti/e, eravate partiti/e, erano partiti/e

**Page 62, Practice 16**

| Io: | avevo mangiato | avevo visto | avevo sentito |
| Tu: | avevi parlato | avevi creduto | avevi pulito |
| Lui, Lei: | aveva visitato | aveva scritto | aveva finito |
| Noi: | eravamo arrivati/e | avevamo bevuto | avevamo capito |
| Voi: | avevate comprato | avevate letto | eravate venuti/e |
| Loro: | avevano dato | avevano potuto | avevano aperto |
| Carlo: | aveva giocato | aveva spinto | aveva costruito |
| Carlo e Maria: | avevano viaggiato | avevano venduto | erano partiti |

**Page 63, Practice 17**

1. avevo capito, 2. eri andato/a, 3. aveva studiato, 4. aveva bevuto, 5. avevamo finito, 6. avevate dormito, 7. avevano comprato, 8. avevo lavorato, 9. avevi pensato, 10. aveva giocato, 11. avevamo viaggiato, 12. avevate pulito, 13. avevano guardato, 14. ero stato/a, 15. eri arrivato/a, 16. era partito, 17. era andata, 18. avevamo letto, 19. avevate scritto, 20. avevamo finito, 21. avevo vinto, 22. aveva perso, 23. era andata, 24. avevamo ascoltato

**Page 64, Practice 18**

1. ho mangiato, 2. avevi mangiato, 3. è andata, 4. era venuto, 5. abbiamo finito, 6. avevamo finito, 7. avete visto, 8. avevate guardato, 9. hanno letto, 10. avevano letto, 11. ho giocato, 12. avevo dormito, 13. ha mangiato, 14. avevamo sciato, 15. non abbiamo letto, 16. non avevamo pensato, 17. non hanno vinto, 18. non avevamo promesso, 19. non ho scelto, 20. non è venuto, 21. non era partita, 22. abbiamo vissuto, 23. non abbiamo vissuto, 24. avevamo vissuto

# Chapter 6

**Page 66, Practice 3**

1. andrei, andresti, andrebbe, andremmo, andreste, andrebbero
2. dovrei, dovresti, dovrebbe, dovremmo, dovreste, dovrebbero
3. verrei, verresti, verrebbe, verremmo, verreste, verrebbero

## Page 67, Practice 4

| Io: | canterei | potrei | capirei |
|---|---|---|---|
| Tu: | balleresti | vedresti | dormiresti |
| Lui, Lei: | nuoterebbe | berrebbe | sentirebbe |
| Noi: | ordineremmo | leggeremmo | finiremmo |
| Voi: | viaggereste | dovreste | partireste |
| Loro: | domanderebbero | vorrebbero | verrebbero |
| Giovanna: | ascolterebbe | avrebbe | direbbe |
| Io e Carlo: | parleremmo | vedremmo | colpiremmo |
| Tu e Giovanna: | desiderereste | vincereste | ubbidireste |
| Giovanna e Carlo: | organizzerebbero | prometterebbero | offrirebbero |

## Page 68, Practice 5

| Io: | non parlerei | non vedrei | non sentirei |
|---|---|---|---|
| Tu: | non viaggeresti | non scriveresti | non puliresti |
| Paolo: | non mangerebbe | non potrebbe | non capirebbe |
| Io e Carlo: | non studieremmo | non leggeremmo | non finiremmo |
| Tu e Paolo: | non arrivereste | non vorreste | non partireste |

## Page 69, Practice 6

1. I would buy, 2. you (s.) would see, 3. I would understand, 4. we wouldn't eat, 5. you (pl.) would come, 6. they would hear, 7. I would study, 8. I wouldn't study, 9. you (s.) would travel, 10. he/she would understand, 11. Carla would arrive, 12. we would be, 13. they would write, 14. I would sleep, 15. you (s.) wouldn't read, 16. Paolo wouldn't leave, 17. we would make/do, 18. you (pl.) would not play, 19. you (pl.) would be, 20. they would listen, 21. I would come, 22. I wouldn't come, 23. you (s.) would stay, 24. Carlo would understand, 25. Maria would cook, 26. we would play, 27. we would want, 28. we wouldn't want, 29. you and Paolo would do/make, 30. I wouldn't do/make, 31. we would go, 32. you (pl.) would bring, 33. Carla couldn't bring, 34. they should, 35. I would invite, 36. they would come

**Interrogative Forms**

1. would you (s.) come?, 2. would they sing?, 3. would he/she understand?, 4. would you (pl.) give?, 5. would he/she speak?, 6. would you (s.) listen?, 7. would we make/do?, 8. would you (s.) cook?

## Page 70, Practice 7

1. penserei, 2. berrei, 3. potresti, 4. farebbe, 5. non farebbe, 6. scriverebbe, 7. lavorerei, 8. berrebbero, 9. pulirei, 10. farebbe, 11. laverebbero, 12. guarderei, 13. vedrebbero, 14. penseremmo, 15. laverei, 16. capiresti, 17. non andrebbero, 18. vedreste, 19. non prenderei, 20. saprei, 21. andresti, 22. non potresti, 23. penserebbe, 24. scriveremmo, 25. leggerebbero, 26. dormirei, 27. non potrebbero, 28. mangeremmo, 29. berrei, 30. viaggereste, 31. ritornerebbe, 32. arriverebbe, 33. partirebbero, 34. non arriverei, 35. non pianterebbe, 36. vincerebbe, 37. mangerebbero, 38. nuoteremmo, 39. sciereste, 40. guarderemmo

## Page 70, Practice 8

1. dovrei andare, 2. dovresti scrivere, 3. dovrebbero studiare, 4. dovremmo venire, 5. dovrebbe cucinare, 6. dovrebbe leggere

## Page 71, Practice 11

1. avrei parlato, avresti parlato, avrebbe parlato, avremmo parlato, avreste parlato, avrebbero parlato
2. avrei visto, avresti visto, avrebbe visto, avremmo visto, avreste visto, avrebbero visto
3. sarei venuto/a, saresti venuto/a, sarebbe venuto/a, saremmo venuti/e, sareste venuti/e, sarebbero venuti/e

**Page 72, Practice 12**

| Io: | sarei andato/a | sarei ritornato/a | sarei partito/a |
|---|---|---|---|
| Tu: | avresti parlato | avresti venduto | avresti capito |
| Lui, Lei: | sarebbe arrivato/a | avrebbe scritto | avrebbe dormito |
| Noi: | avremmo informato | avremmo letto | avremmo preferito |
| Voi: | avreste aspettato | avreste dovuto | avreste finito |
| Loro: | avrebbero abitato | avrebbero bevuto | sarebbero usciti/e |
| Carlo: | avrebbe invitato | avrebbe voluto | avrebbe sentito |

**Page 73, Practice 13**

1. I would have waited, 2. you (s.) would talk, 3. he/she would have eaten, 4. they would understand, 5. you (pl.) would write, 6. you (pl.) would have written, 7. they would answer, 8. he/she would not have answered, 9. I would hear, 10. I would have heard, 11. we would have signed, 12. I would invite, 13. you (pl.) would go out, 14. we would finish, 15. they would have finished, 16. you (pl.) would buy, 17. he would buy, 18. you (s.) would find, 19. I would have looked, 20. he/she would answer, 21. he/she would have answered, 22. you (pl.) would have written, 23. I would know, 24. he/she would have known

**Page 74, Practice 14**

1. andrei, 2. avresti preso, 3. avremmo ballato, 4. sarebbero venuti/e, 5. saprebbe, 6. aspetteremmo, 7. avremmo cominciato, 8. scriverebbe, 9. avrebbe risposto, 10. parlerebbero, 11. sarebbero dovuti/e venire, 12. avrei dovuto parlare, 13. dovrebbe aspettare, 14. avrebbe dovuto aspettare, 15. capiremmo, 16. avrebbero capito, 17. avrebbe scritto, 18. avresti risposto, 19. avresti dovuto rispondere, 20. viaggerebbero, 21. sarei ritornato, 22. sarebbe partito, 23. arriverebbe, 24. partiremmo

# Chapter 7

**Page 78, Practice 4**

1. domandi, domandi, domandi, domandiamo, domandiate, domandino
2. veda, veda, veda, vediamo, vediate, vedano
3. senta, senta, senta, sentiamo, sentiate, sentano
4. capisca, capisca, capisca, capiamo, capiate, capiscano
5. giochi, giochi, giochi, giochiamo, giochiate, giochino
6. paghi, paghi, paghi, paghiamo, paghiate, paghino

**Page 79, Practice 5**

| Che io: | domandi | decida | senta |
|---|---|---|---|
| Che tu: | compri | veda | finisca |
| Che lui: | prepari | legga | capisca |
| Che lei: | aspetti | comprenda | pulisca |
| Che noi: | arriviamo | accendiamo | diciamo |
| Che voi: | visitiate | beviate | partiate |
| Che loro: | lavorino | chiudano | capiscano |

**Page 80, Practice 6**

| Io voglio che tu: | mangi | legga | parta |
|---|---|---|---|
| Io voglio che lui: | parli | perda | offra |
| Io voglio che lei: | stia | discuta | apra |
| Io spero che noi: | impariamo | sorridiamo | capiamo |
| Io desidero che voi: | facciate | vediate | ridiate |
| Io penso che loro: | desiderino | debbano | ubbidiscano |
| Io voglio: | visitare | vincere | capire |
| Loro vogliono: | visitare | arrivare | partire |

## Page 81, Practice 7

1. legga, 2. studino, 3. comprino, 4. capisca, 5. venga, 6. arrivino, 7. finisca, 8. venga, 9. possa, 10. legga, 11. veniamo, 12. pensiate, 13. sapere, 14. ritorni, 15. sappia, 16. vada, 17. vinca, 18. perda, 19. pensino, 20. controlli, 21. possano, 22. sapere, 23. puliscano, 24. comprare

## Page 82, Practice 8

1. che io vada, 2. che lui senta, 3. che noi mangiamo, 4. che loro parlino, 5. che voi sentiate, 6. che tu beva, 7. che lei parta, 8. che lui capisca, 9. che noi lavoriamo, 10. che voi sentiate, 11. che voi ascoltiate, 12. che loro leggano, 13. che voi non ascoltiate, 14. che voi andiate, 15. che io parta, 16. che lui arrivi, 17. che piova, 18. che io sappia, 19. che tu conosca, 20. che tu possa, 21. che voi non leggiate, 22. che voi compriate, 23. che voi vendiate, 24. che voi capiate

## Page 83, Practice 9

1. vada, 2. partire, 3. arrivi, 4. pensi, 5. visiti, 6. andare, 7. capisca, 8. comprare, 9. veda, 10. possa, 11. vogliamo, 12. legga, 13. finire, 14. paghi, 15. ascolti, 16. compri, 17. vendiamo, 18. scriva, 19. guardino, 20. studi, 21. parta, 22. rimaniamo, 23. perdiate, 24. rimanga

## Page 85, Practice 12

1. che io ascoltassi, che tu ascoltassi, che lui ascoltasse, che lei ascoltasse, che noi ascoltassimo, che voi ascoltaste, che loro ascoltassero
2. che io conoscessi, che tu conoscessi, che lui conoscesse, che lei conoscesse, che noi conoscessimo, che voi conosceste, che loro conoscessero
3. che io venissi, che tu venissi, che lui venisse, che lei venisse, che noi venissimo, che voi veniste, che loro venissero

## Page 86, Practice 13

| Che io: | parlassi | leggessi | pulissi |
| Che tu: | comprassi | vedessi | finissi |
| Che lui: | andasse | potesse | sentisse |
| Che lei: | arrivasse | corresse | partisse |
| Che noi: | dimenticassimo | bevessimo | dormissimo |
| Che voi: | perdonaste | scriveste | veniste |
| Che loro: | studiassero | temessero | capissero |

## Page 87, Practice 14

| Pensavo che tu: | facessi | vincessi | capissi |
| Pensavo che lui: | lavorasse | perdesse | finisse |
| Pensavo che lei: | studiasse | correggesse | sentisse |
| Pensavo che noi: | cambiassimo | sapessimo | dormissimo |
| Pensavo che voi: | sognaste | accendeste | costruiste |
| Pensavo che loro: | insegnassero | spegnessero | venissero |
| Speravo che tu: | parlassi | vedessi | finissi |
| Speravo che voi: | faceste | leggeste | puliste |

## Page 88, Practice 15

1. volevo che tu venissi, 2. speravo che tu venissi, 3. pensavi di poter studiare, 4. pensavi che lui studiasse, 5. pensavi che venissimo, 6. speravo che voi veniste, 7. credevo che scrivesse, 8. pensavo che andassimo, 9. speravi che chiamassero, 10. pensavano che rimanessi, 11. tutti voi pensavate che giocasse, 12. pensavo che tu pulissi, 13. non sapevo che tu andassi, 14. volevi che io cucinassi, 15. vorrebbe che tu leggessi, 16. sarebbe necessario che tu partissi, 17. mio padre voleva che io lavorassi, 18. era difficile che tu andassi, 19. non sapevo che tu fossi cosi alto/a, 20. voleva che chiedessi al dottore, 21. volevo dormire tutto il giorno, 22. volevo che dormisse tutto il giorno, 23, voleva che andassimo, 24. speravo che mi invitassero

1. parli, 2. parlassi, 3. veniamo, 4. venissimo, 5. sia, 6. fosse, 7. studi, 8. studiasse, 9. studiate, 10. studiaste, 11. venire, 12. venire, 13. impari, 14. imparasse, 15. sogni, 16. sognassi, 17. facciano, 18. facessero, 19. ricordiate, 20. ricordasse, 21. arrivi, 22. arrivasse, 23. scriva, 24. scrivessi

# Chapter 8

### Page 91, Practice 3

| Che io: | sia arrivato/a | abbia visto | abbia finito |
| Che tu: | abbia parlato | abbia letto | abbia capito |
| Che lui: | abbia ascoltato | abbia scritto | abbia sentito |
| Che lei: | abbia piantato | sia scesa | sia salita |
| Che noi: | abbiamo studiato | abbiamo venduto | abbiamo sostituito |
| Che voi: | abbiate cancellato | abbiate bevuto | siate venuti/e |
| Che loro: | abbiano guardato | abbiano mantenuto | siano partiti/e |
| Che io: | non abbia sperato | non abbia aspettato | non abbia riso |

### Page 92, Practice 4

1. sia venuto, 2. abbia parlato, 3. abbiamo studiato, 4. abbia perso, 5. siamo andati/e, 6. abbia pagato, 7. abbia arrestato, 8. abbia trovato, 9. abbiate mangiato, 10. sia partita, 11. abbia telefonato, 12. abbiate telefonato, 13. abbia studiato, 14. siano venuti/e, 15. abbiate nuotato, 16. sia ritornato/a, 17. abbia finito, 18. abbia capito, 19. abbia trovato, 20. sia partito, 21. abbia scritto, 22. abbiano studiato, 23. abbia studiato, 24. abbia telefonato

### Page 93, Practice 5

| 1. parli | parlassi | abbia parlato |
| 2. senta | sentissi | abbia sentito |
| 3. capisca | capisse | abbia capito |
| 4. venga | venisse | sia venuta |
| 5. offriamo | offrissimo | abbiamo offerto |
| 6. prendiate | prendeste | aveste preso |
| 7. vedano | vedessero | abbiano visto |
| 8. pensi | pensassi | abbia pensato |
| 9. legga | leggessi | abbia letto |
| 10. pulisca | pulisse | abbia pulito |
| 11. stiamo | stessimo | siamo stati |

### Page 94, Practice 8

1. That I had arrived
2. That you (s.) had thought
3. That we had left
4. That you (pl.) had spoken
5. That they had come

### Page 95, Practice 9

1. Sembrava che avesse saputo tutto, 2. era possibile che fosse arrivata, 3. speravamo che fosse entrata, 4. pensavo che fosse arrivato, 5. dubitavo che avessi saputo, 6. sembrava che avesse capito, 7. era meglio che fossi andato/a, 8. era meglio che fossero partiti/e, 9. sembrava che io avessi saputo, 10. preferivo che foste andati/e, 11. preferivamo che tu avessi studiato, 12. ero sicuro che Carlo fosse arrivato, 13. preferiva che avessimo imparato, 14. ero contento che tu fossi venuto/a, 15. eravamo sicuri che fossero partiti/e, 16. era probabile che fossi arrivato/a, 17. pensavo che tu fossi venuto/a, 18. dubitavo che avesse trovato lavoro, 19. credevo che avesse cercato lavoro, 20. era necessario che io avessi letto, 21. era bene che avessero comprato, 22. era necessario che avessero venduto, 23. speravo che Carlo avesse venduto

**Page 96, Practice 12**

1. spiegassi, 2 potessi, 3. avessimo, 4. sapesse, 5. guidasse, 6. avessi spiegato, 7. avesse potuto, 8. avessimo avuto, 9. avesse saputo, 10. avesse guidato, 11. avesse venduto, 12. avessi saputo, 13. avessi potuto, 14. aveste studiato

**Page 99, Practice 16**

| Io: | mi alzo | mi metto | mi sento |
| --- | --- | --- | --- |
| Tu: | ti addormenti | ti pettini | ti domandi |
| Lui: | si lava | si pettina | si veste |
| Lei: | si diverte | si sposa | si prepara |
| Noi: | ci vestiamo | ci svegliamo | ci aiutiamo |
| Voi: | vi parlate | vi salutate | vi incontrate |
| Loro: | si divertono | si sposano | si preparano |

**Page 100, Practice 17**

1. he wakes up, 2. she gets dressed, 3. they get ready, 4. we get ready, 5. you (pl.) greet each other, 6. they talk to each other, 7. you (pl.) hate each other, 8. they love each other, 9. he/she begins to talk, 10. they write each other, 11. I get up, 12. you wash yourself, 13. he washes himself, 14. Carlo gets dressed, 15. we meet each other, 16. I get dressed, 17. he/she falls asleep, 18. you (pl.) talk to each other, 19. they help each other, 20. I fall asleep, 21. he combs his hair, 22. they look at themselves in the mirror, 23. you (pl.) get ready, 24. they kneel

**Page 101, Practice 18**

1. ci svegliamo, 2. mi diverto, 3. si alzano, 4. si svegliano, 5. si salutano, 6. si preparano, 7. si lava, 8. si pettina, 9. si incontrano, 10. si divertono, 11. si diverte, 12. si prepara, 13. vi vestite, 14. mi vesto, 15. ci aiutiamo, 16. ci alziamo, 17. ci svegliamo, 18. ci amiamo, 19. ci siamo svegliati, 20. si è alzato, 21. ti sei lavato/a, 22. si è pettinata, 23. si sono odiati/e, 24. si è divertito

# Chapter 9

**Page 103, Practice 3**

**A.** 1. sto parlando, 2. stai ascoltando, 3 stiamo parlando, 4. sta guidando, 5. sta sentendo, 6. stiamo studiando, 7. state partendo, 8. stai leggendo, 9. sta parlando, 10. sto giocando, 11. stai partendo, 12. stanno tornando

**B.** 1. stavi andando, 2. stavi ascoltando, 3. stavate parlando, 4. stavo bevendo, 5. stavate vedendo, 6. stavamo giocando, 7. stavate scrivendo, 8. stava leggendo, 9. stavi prendendo, 10. stavo bevendo, 11. stavi partendo, 12. stavo tornando

**Page 106, Practice 6**

| I want to go | I must study | I can bring |
| --- | --- | --- |
| we wanted to leave | we had to arrive | we could hear |
| he/she will want to bring | he/she will have to run | he/she will be able to buy |
| they wanted to listen | they had to do | they could tell |
| they wanted to come | they had to go | they could leave |

**Page 106, Practice 7**

| voglio pensare | devo andare | posso cantare |
| --- | --- | --- |
| volevi scrivere | dovevi vedere | potevi leggere |
| vorremmo venire | dovremmo comprare | potremmo vendere |
| hanno voluto giocare | hanno dovuto chiudere | avrebbero potuto pulire |

**Page 107, Practice 8**

1. when was the bill paid?, 2. by whom was the Divine Comedy written? 3. America was discovered in 1492, 4. the boy was woken up, 5. the house is finished

**Page 107, Practice 9**

1. l'inglese è studiato da molti, 2. la partita è stata giocata sotto la pioggia, 3. quando è stato trovato il cane? 4. la casa è pulita da Paolo, 5. la macchina è stata venduta in fretta

**Page 109, Practice 10**

**Present**
1. disdico, 2. rifai, 3. fraintendete, 4. intervengono, 5. tolgo, 6. rifa, 7. suppongono, 8. ottiene, 9. interdicono, 10. rivediamo

**Future**
1. rifarò, 2. contenderanno, 3. supporrà, 4. prevedremo, 5. rifarete, 6. opporremo, 7. otterranno, 8. predirò, 9. contraddirà, 10. interverranno

**Passato Remoto**
1. addivennero, 2. previde, 3. soddisfecero, 4. predicemmo, 5. tolsi, 6. fraintendeste, 7. propose, 8. contraddissero, 9. prevenisti, 10. contraffecero

**Passato Prossimo**
1. ho stupefatto, 2. hai opposto, 3. abbiamo disdetto, 4. hanno previsto, 5. ha ottenuto, 6. hai preteso

**Page 110, Practice 11**

1. predissero, 2. distenderemo, 3. diviene, 4. perverremo, 5. interdirà, 6. supposero, 7. contraffanno, 8. preveniamo, 9. prevedrà, 10. opponi, 11. soddisfaranno, 12. fraintendete, 13. raccolse, 14. contradici, 15. contendemmo, 16. toglierò, 17. stupefaranno, 18. avvide, 19. rifaccio, 20. distendeste, 21. supponiamo, 22. proposi, 23. distogliamo, 24. raccoglie, 25. disdirò, 26. contraffaremo, 27. opponi, 28. diveniste, 29. togliemmo, 30. intervenne

# Chapter 10

**Page 111, Practice 1**

| Io: | parlo | vedo | sento | capisco |
|-----|-------|------|-------|---------|
| Tu: | cammini | scrivi | parti | finisci |
| Lui: | lavora | legge | viene | pulisce |
| Lei: | cucina | teme | dice | esce |
| Noi: | insegniamo | vogliamo | scopriamo | offriamo |
| Voi: | arrivate | vincete | avvenite | riuscite |
| Loro: | cambiano | perdono | muoiono | salgono |

**Page 112, Practice 2**

cominciavo, parlavi, arrivava, mangiava
perdeva, vinceva, dicevamo, davano
venivamo, capivi, finiva, salivo
parlavo, diventavi, comprava, passavamo
leggevi, eravamo, scrivevate, dovevano
finivamo, dicevate, capivano, finivi
chiudevo, arrivavi, partiva, usciva
cambiavamo, scrivevate, entravano, fuggivi
avevo, dovevi, andavamo, era
potevamo, facevi, usciva, volevano
venivano, diceva, uscivano, finiva
andavo, capivano, finivate, partivi

**Page 113, Practice 3**

**A.** 1. I'll eat, 2. you'll (s.) hear, 3. he'll climb, 4. we'll buy, 5. we'll make/do, 6. I'll study, 7. I'll hear, 8. he/she listens, 9. you'll (pl.) leave, 10. you'll (pl.) understand, 11. I'll make/do, 12. you'll (s.) want, 13. you'll (pl.) have to, 14. you'll (pl.) get up, 15. I'll drive, 16. we'll fly, 17. you'll (s.) stop, 18. I'll know, 19. I'll know, 20. we'll arrive, 21. I'll stay, 22. we'll be, 23. you'll (pl.) read

**B.** 1. andrò, 2. dormirai, 3. mangerà, 4. pulirò, 5. camminerà, 6. chiamerete, 7. ascolterò, 8. cambierai, 9. staremo, 10. entreranno, 11. riderò, 12. potremo, 13. vedrò, 14. andrete, 15. scriveranno, 16. risponderà, 17. dovrò, 18. dimenticherò, 19. pulirà, 20. staranno, 21. farò, 22. chiuderà, 23. berranno

**Page 114, Practice 4**

|      | Passato Remoto | Passato Prossimo |
|------|----------------|------------------|
| Io:  | andai          | sono andato/a    |
| Tu:  | facesti        | hai fatto        |
| Lui: | venne          | è venuto         |
| Lei: | capì           | ha capito        |
| Noi: | vedemmo        | abbiamo visto    |
| Voi: | pensaste       | avete pensato    |
| Loro:| sentirono      | hanno sentito    |
| Io:  | stetti         | sono stato/a     |
| Tu:  | chiedesti      | hai chiesto      |
| Lui: | mandò          | ha mandato       |
| Lei: | pensò          | ha pensato       |

**Page 115, Practice 5**

**A.** 1. I had eaten, 2. we had understood, 3. they had slept, 4. they had left, 5. I had gone, 6. we had been, 7. we had spoken, 8. you (s.) had studied, 9. I had understood, 10. I had closed, 11. you (s.) had heard, 12. we had brought, 13. he had lost, 14. you (pl.) had won, 15. I had telephoned, 16. she had finished, 17. I had been, 18. they had climbed, 19. she had descended, 20. you (pl.) had left, 21. we had been sorry, 22. they had died, 23. I had entered

**B.** 1. avevo dormito, 2. era entrato, 3. aveva parlato, 4. avevamo capito, 5. avevate fatto, 6. aveva fatto, 7. aveva scritto, 8. eri stato/a, 9. aveva visto, 10. eravamo venuti/e, 11. erano ritornati/e, 12. eravamo andati/e, 13. avevo mangiato, 14. avevi scritto, 15. avevano pulito, 16. avevamo letto, 17. aveva messo, 18. avevamo detto, 19. avevo saputo, 20. aveva visto, 21. avevo voluto, 22. avevate detto, 23. era nata

**Page 116, Practice 6**

1. vorrei (mi piacerebbe), 2. leggerei, 3. parlereste, 4. ascolterebbe, 5. pulirei, 6. scriverebbero, 7. penseremmo, 8. risponderei, 9. leggeresti, 10. mangerebbe, 11. venderebbe, 12. studieremmo, 13. scierei, 14. viaggerebbero, 15. berreste, 16. studierei, 17. dovrei, 18. potrei, 19. vorresti, 20. penseremmo, 21. chiuderebbero, 22. apriremmo, 23. capirebbe

**Page 117, Practice 7**

1. avrei voluto (mi sarebbe piaciuto), 2. sarei stato/a, 3. avrebbe parlato, 4. avrei ascoltato, 5. avreste pulito, 6. avrebbero scritto, 7. avrebbero pensato, 8. avrebbe letto, 9. avremmo mangiato, 10. sarebbero arrivati/e, 11. sarei stato/a, 12. saremmo stati/e, 13. avresti bevuto, 14. avrebbe studiato, 15. sarebbe andata, 16. avreste voluto, 17. avrei chiuso, 18. avrebbe aperto, 19. avrebbe pensato, 20. avremmo capito, 21. avrebbero viaggiato, 22. avresti cantato, 23. avrebbero guardato, 24. saremmo venuti/e

**Page 118, Practice 8**

| Present Subjunctive | Imperfect Subjunctive |
|---|---|
| 1. mangi | mangiassi |
| 2. veda | vedessi |
| 3. parli | parlasse |
| 4. senta | sentisse |
| 5. chiudiamo | chiudessimo |
| 6. capiate | capiste |
| 7. vengano | venissero |
| 8. rispondiamo | rispondessimo |
| 9. scriva | scrivessi |
| 10. impari | imparassi |
| 11. finisca | finisse |
| 12. mangiamo | mangiassimo |
| 13. beviate | beveste |
| 14. sappiano | sapessero |
| 15. telefoni | telefonassi |
| 16. prenda | prendesse |
| 17. stiate | steste |
| 18. stia | stessi |
| 19. dobbiate | doveste |
| 20. capiscano | capissero |
| 21. legga | leggesse |
| 22. mandi | mandassi |
| 23. venda | vendesse |

**Page 119, Practice 9**

| 1. sia venuto/a | fossi venuto/a |
|---|---|
| 2. abbia parlato | avesse parlato |
| 3. abbiamo ascoltato | avessimo ascoltato |
| 4. abbia fatto | avesse fatto |
| 5. abbiate finito | aveste finito |
| 6. siate andati/e | foste andati/e |
| 7. abbiano chiuso | avessero chiuso |
| 8. abbia aperto | avessi aperto |
| 9. abbia potuto | avessi potuto |
| 10. abbia detto | avesse detto |
| 11. abbiamo finito | avessimo finito |
| 12. abbia capito | avessi capito |
| 13. abbia risposto | avessi risposto |
| 14. abbia visto | avesse visto |
| 15. abbiate parlato | aveste parlato |
| 16. abbia vissuto | avessi vissuto |
| 17. abbia preso | avesse preso |
| 18. abbiano viaggiato | avessero viaggiato |
| 19. abbia ordinato | avessi ordinato |
| 20. abbiate insegnato | aveste insegnato |
| 21. abbia bevuto | avessi bevuto |
| 22. abbia aspettato | avesse aspettato |
| 23. abbia ricevuto | avessi ricevuto |

**Page 120, Practice 10**

|       | Present    | Future     | Imperfect  | Passato Remoto |
|-------|------------|------------|------------|----------------|
| Io:   | faccio     | farò       | facevo     | feci           |
| Tu:   | vai        | andrai     | andavi     | andasti        |
| Lui:  | mangia     | mangerà    | mangiava   | mangiò         |
| Lei:  | parla      | parlerà    | parlava    | parlò          |
| Noi:  | leggiamo   | leggeremo  | leggevamo  | leggemmo       |
| Voi:  | bevete     | berrete    | bevevate   | beveste        |
| Loro: | vedono     | vedranno   | vedevano   | videro         |
| Io:   | sento      | sentirò    | sentivo    | sentii         |
| Lui:  | dà         | darà       | dava       | diede          |
| Voi:  | state      | starete    | stavate    | steste         |
| Lei:  | capisce    | capirà     | capiva     | capì           |
| Loro: | finiscono  | finiranno  | finivano   | finirono       |
| Io:   | rispondo   | risponderò | rispondevo | risposi        |
| Lui:  | pulisce    | pulirà     | puliva     | pulì           |
| Noi:  | arriviamo  | arriveremo | arrivavamo | arrivammo      |
| Voi:  | salite     | salirete   | salivate   | saliste        |
| Tu:   | soffri     | soffrirai  | soffrivi   | soffristi      |
| Lei:  | offre      | offrià     | offriva    | offrì          |
| Io:   | imparo     | imparerò   | imparavo   | imparai        |
| Loro: | vede       | vedrà      | vedeva     | vide           |
| Lei:  | cade       | cadrà      | cadeva     | cadde          |
| Lui:  | muore      | morirà     | moriva     | morì           |

**Page 121, Practice 11**

1. ho capito — avevo capito
2. hai visto — avevi visto
3. ha finito — aveva finito
4. ha letto — aveva letto
5. siamo ritornati/e — eravamo ritornati/e
6. avete imparato — avevate imparato
7. hanno cenato — avevano cenato
8. ho pranzato — avevo pranzato
9. ha venduto — aveva venduto
10. ha acceso — aveva acceso
11. avete accettato — avevate accettato
12. hanno spento — avevano spento
13. ho lavato — avevo lavato
14. siamo usciti/e — eravamo usciti/e
15. hai viaggiato — avevi viaggiato
16. è partito — era partito
17. ha guarito — aveva guarito
18. siete arrivati/e — eravate arrivati/e
19. hai ascoltato — avevi ascoltato
20. hanno saltato — avevano saltato
21. ha esaminato — aveva esaminato
22. abbiamo diviso — avevamo diviso
23. ha stirato — aveva stirato

## Page 122, Practice 12

| | | |
|---|---|---|
| 1. | parlerei | avrei parlato |
| 2. | arriveresti | saresti arrivato/a |
| 3. | canterebbe | avrebbe cantato |
| 4. | laverebbe | avrebbe lavato |
| 5. | lavorerebbe | avrebbe lavorato |
| 6. | staremmo | saremmo stati/e |
| 7. | andreste | sareste andati/e |
| 8. | viaggerebbero | avrebbero viaggiato |
| 9. | vedrei | avrei visto |
| 10. | potresti | avresti potuto |
| 11. | leggerebbe | avrebbe letto |
| 12. | scriverebbe | avrebbe scritto |
| 13. | correremmo | saremmo corsi/e |
| 14. | rispondereste | avreste risposto |
| 15. | cadrebbero | sarebbero caduti/e |
| 16. | capirei | avrei capito |
| 17. | finiresti | avresti finito |
| 18. | verrebbe | sarebbe venuto |
| 19. | sentiremmo | avremmo sentito |
| 20. | offrireste | avreste offerto |
| 21. | pulirebbero | avrebbero pulito |

## Page 123, Practice 13

| | Present | Imperfect | Past | Pluperfect Subjunctive |
|---|---|---|---|---|
| Io: | vada | andassi | sia andato/a | fossi andato/a |
| Tu: | ritorni | ritornassi | sia ritornato/a | fossi ritornato/a |
| Lui: | dia | desse | abbia dato | avesse dato |
| Lei: | faccia | facesse | abbia fatto | avesse fatto |
| Noi: | stiamo | stessimo | siamo stati/e | fossimo stati/e |
| Voi: | beviate | beveste | abbiate bevuto | aveste bevuto |
| Loro: | vedano | vedessero | abbiano visto | avessero visto |
| Noi: | fermiamo | fermassimo | abbiamo fermato | avessimo fermato |
| Lui: | senta | sentisse | abbia sentito | avesse sentito |
| Lei: | divida | dividesse | abbia diviso | avesse diviso |
| Lui: | paghi | pagasse | abbia pagato | avesse pagato |
| Tu: | venda | vendessi | abbia venduto | avessi venduto |
| Io: | dorma | dormissi | abbia dormito | avessi dormito |
| Loro: | contino | contassero | abbiano contato | avessero contato |
| Voi: | diciate | diceste | abbiate detto | aveste detto |
| Lei: | giochi | giocasse | abbia giocato | avesse giocato |
| Lui: | salti | saltasse | abbia saltato | avesse saltato |
| Noi: | guardiamo | guardassimo | abbiamo guardato | avessimo guardato |
| Tu: | salga | salissi | sia salito/a | fossi salito/a |
| Voi: | leggiate | leggeste | abbiate letto | aveste letto |
| Loro: | tirino | tirassero | abbiano tirato | avessero tirato |
| Noi: | pensiamo | pensassimo | abbiamo pensato | avessimo pensato |

# Chapter 11

## Page 125, Practice 2

1. ho bisogno di scarpe, 2. ho caldo, 3. hai freddo, 4. abbiamo fretta, 5. hammo mal di testa, 6. ho paura, 7. ha sete, 8. aveva sonno, 9. avevano ragione, 10. avevo torto, 11. abbiamo vergogna, 12. ho voglia di mangiare, 13. avevate fame, 14. avevano fretta, 15. avrei sete, 16. avrebbero bisogno di scarpe, 17. avrebbe ragione, 18. avremmo torto, 19. avrei paura, 20. avrebbe intenzione, 21. ho avuto mal di testa, 22. hanno avuto paura, 23. abbiamo avuto paura

## Page 128, Practice 4

1. facciamo alla romana, 2. fa attenzione, 3. faccio calazione, 4. facciamo un bagno, 5. hanno fatto una crociera, 6. fa la spesa, 7. ti sei fatto/a male, 8. faccio un favore, 9. fanno una passeggiata, 10. farò fotografie, 11. ha fatto un viaggio, 12. fate una domanda, 13. fa uno spuntino, 14. facciamo in fretta, 15. fa caldo, 16. facciamo un regalo, 17. facciamo una visita, 18. faceva freddo, 19. fa la predica, 20. farà un discorso, 21. fanno quattro chicciere, 22. ha fatto brutta figura

## Page 133, Practice 10

1. We learn to ski, 2. I start to understand, 3. I forgot to study, 4. I'm thinking of coming, 5. he/she needs to study, 6. he/she thought about you, 7. we'll stay home, 8. they'll return to Rome, 9. I am afraid of everything, 10. they wait to come, 11. I need you, 12. she continues to eat, 13. he/she used to teach driving, 14. you (pl.) hope you see, 15. I realize I'm late, 16. he/she falls in love with everybody, 17. I don't trust him, 18. she lives on love, 19. stop (s.) talking, 20. you count (pl.) on your sister, 21. he/she tried walking, 22. he/she pretends to look in the book, 23. we laugh at him, 24. they give thanks for everything

## Page 134, Practice 11

1. vado a ballare, 2. andiamo a studiare, 3. sei stato/a a Roma?, 4. credo nei fantasmi, 5. pensano alle vacanze, 6. proverò a venire, 7. pensiamo di andare, 8. ti insegnerò a nuotare, 9. finisco de lavorare, 10. ha voglia de mangiare cioccolata, 11. comincio a parlare, 12. si ferma a Parigi, 13. cerchiamo di venire, 14. chiamami prima de partire, 15. continui a studiare, 16. hanno promesso di andare, 17. ho promesso di venire, 18. hanno bisogno di pensare, 19. sperate di dormire, 20. hanno voglia de viaggiare, 21. smetti di parlare, 22. fanno attenzione all'insegnante

# Chapter 12

## Page 135, *-are* Verbs

### abitare

1. Dove abiti? Abito a Napoli. 2. Abitano in Italia da molto tempo. 3. Quando ero giovane, abitavo in Florida. 4. Vorrebbe abitare in una casa grande. 5. Spera di abitare vicino al mare.

### addormentare

6. Questo film mi fa addormentare. 7. La donna si è addormentata sul divano. 8. Questa lezione mi fa addormentare. 9. Io mi addormento con la luce accesa.

### addormentarsi

10. Paolo si addormenta davanti alla televisione. 11. Non addormentarti al cinema. 12. Il bambino si è addormentato subito.

### alzare (qualche cosa)

13. Per favore, alza il riscaldamento. 14. Dovrebbe alzare la voce, nessuno lo sente.

### alzarsi

15. Il giovane si alza sempre tardi. 16. In inverno, il sole si alza tardi.

### andare

17. Vanno a scuola alle otto. 18. Dove sei andato ieri sera? 19. Vorrei che lei andasse all'università. 20. È andata a Roma con me. 21. A marzo andremo in Italia.

### andare a

22. Non vado a scuola questa sera. 23. Vorresti andare a ballare? 24. Il prossimo mese andrò a visitare degli amici. 25. Potresti andare all'ufficio postale? 26. La prossima settimana andrò al museo. 27. Lei vorrebbe andare a sciare con noi.

**andare da + article**

28. È andata dal dottore. 29. Vorrei andare dal macellaio. 30. Penso che siano andati dal loro amico.

**andare in**

31. Il prossimo anno vorrei andare in Italia. 32. Andrà in Cina con degli amici. 33. Andranno in macchina o in aereo? 34. Mia mamma è andata in cucina.

**arrivare**

35. I miei amici arriveranno domani. 36. Il tuo biglietto è arrivato ieri. 37. Spero (che) siano arrivati bene.

**arrivare a**

38. Sono arrivati all'aereoporto. 39. Arriverò a Venezia fra una settimana.

**arrivare in**

40. Sono arrivati in America con la nave. 41. Ha detto che è arrivata in Cina. 42. Vorrei arrivare in Grecia in estate. 43. Arriverò domani in macchina.

**arrivare in**

44. Siamo arrivati negli Stati Uniti. 45. I turisti arrivano in estate.

**aspettare**

46. Aspetto mia sorella. 47. L'ho aspettato per tanto tempo.

**chiamare**

48. Hanno chiamato un tassi un'ora fa. 49. Sta molto male, dobbiamo chiamare il dottore. 50. Vogliono chiamarla, ma è troppo tardi.

**chiamarsi**

51. Non so come ti chiami. 52. Come si chiama tua sorella? Si chiama Carla.

**dare**

53. Gli ho dato un libro. 54. Sperava (che) gli dessero il primo premio. 55. Potresti darmi la tua macchina sabato? 56. Il presidente ha dato le dimissioni. 57. Mi ha dato tanti soldi.

**desiderare**

58. Il bambino desidera molti regali per Natale. 59. Carlo desidera parlarti. 60. Desideri vedere qualche cosa? 61. Al ristorante desiderava provare tutto. 62. Desideri una tazza di caffè o (di) tè? 63. Desideriamo che tu venga a visitarci.

**diventare**

64. Carla è diventata alta. 65. Verdi è diventato molto famoso. 66. La gente in Italia sta diventando molto vecchia. 67. È diventata una bella ragazza.

**fare**

68. Che cosa mi suggerisci di fare? 69. Tutti i giorni lei fa i biscotti. 70. Ha fatto un bel vestito. 71. Vorrei fare la maestra. 72. Ieri faceva molto freddo. 73. In estate fa molto caldo. 74. Spero (che) farai una bella vacanza. 75. Stanno facendo una strada nuova. 76. Sperava di fare una lunga passeggiata. 77. L'artista ha fatto una bella statua.

**guardare**

78. L'insegnante lo guarda. 79. Hai guardato il suo compito? 80. Mi guardava fisso.

**mandare**

81. Manda a letto i bambini. 82. Ha mandato a letto i bambini. 83. Manderò il pacco per posta. 84. Speravo (che) tu mi mandassi il tuo libro. 85. Devi mandare il libro per posta. 86. Ti mando un bacio.

**pensare**

87. Penso (che) sia troppo freddo per uscire. 88. Pensa chi ho visto ieri sera? 89. Avrebbero dovuto pensarci.

**sognare**

90. Ho sognato che volavo. 91. Giovanna sognava ad occhi aperti. 92. Non avrei mai sognato di vincere la lotteria.

**stare**

93. I bambini vogliono stare dentro oggi. 94. Starò in Italia per due settimane. 95. Bambini, state zitti! 96. Mia madre stava alla finestra. 97. I miei amici stanno a Roma.


## Page 140, *-ere* Verbs

**accendere**

1. Accendi la luce, per piacere. 2. Non voglio che tu accenda la sigaretta.

**avere**

3. Suo figlio ha l'influenza. 4. I loro parenti non hanno soldi per vivere. 5. L'avrei fatto, se avessi avuto tempo. 6. Avevano molti amici. 7. Hai fame? Sì, ho molta fame. 8. Quel bambino ha molta fortuna. 9. La mia amica ha sempre fretta. 10. La donna aveva un bel vestito.

**bere**

11. Quell'uomo beve troppo. 12. Beviamo alla nostra salute. 13. Penso (che) gli piaccia bere vino rosso.

**chiedere**

14. Mi ha chiesto aiuto. 15. Mia madre chiede sempre di te. 16. Quanto chiedi per questa casa?

**chiudere**

17. I negozi chiudono alle 7:30. 18. Non chiudi mai la porta. 19. Hai chiuso la bottiglia? 20. L'ho chiuso fuori di casa.

**conoscere**

21. Tuo padre conosce bene l'Italia. 22. Conosci un bravo dottore? 23. Ho conosciuto mio marito in Africa. 24. Non la conosco bene.

**correre**

25. Quel bambino correva come il vento. 26. Il treno corre velocemente. 27. Dobbiamo correre per prendere l'autobus. 28. I bambini non possono correre in piscina.

**credere a, in**

29. Nessuno lo crede. 30. Paolo non crede in Dio.

**credere che**

31. Non credevo (che) fossero già arrivati. 32. Crede che domani pioverà.

**decidere di**

33. Non posso decidere quando andare in Italia. 34. Ha deciso di rispettare le regole della scuola. 35. Decideranno presto dove andare in vacanza.

**difendere**

36. Lei difende sempre suo fratello. 37. I soldati hanno difeso la città dai nemici. 38. I guanti difendono le mani dal freddo.

**dispiacere**

39. Ti dispiacerebbe se venissi a casa con te? 40. Mi dispiace non poterti visitare. 41. Se non ti dispiace, vorrei riposare. 42. Mi dispiace che tua mamma non sia potuta venire.

**dovere**

43. Che cosa dovrei fare? 44. Non dovrei dirti questa storia. 45. Carlo è diventato un grande scrittore. 46. Non devi comprarlo oggi.

**essere**

47. Di dove sei? Sei americano? 48. Che ore sono? È presto o è tardi? 49. Paolo non è in casa. 50. Che sarà, sarà. 51. Non è possibile che vengano. 52. Non era possibile che venissero. 53. Che cosa è successo?

**mettere**

54. Mettiamo tutti i libri sulla scrivania. 55. Abbiamo messo le tende sulle finestre. 56. Hai messo via le valige?

**mettersi**

57. Si è messa il suo nuovo costume da bagno. 58. Si è messa a piangere. 59. Si è messo vicino alla finestra.

**nascere**

60. Mio figlio è nato il 12 ottobre. 61. Credi che io sia nata ieri? 62. Tua sorella è nata a Venezia. 63. Il sole si alza a est. 64. Nascono come i funghi.

**rispondere**

65. Spero che tu risponderai alla mia lettera. 66. Perchè non hai risposto? 67. Nessuno risponde al telefono.

**rispondere di**

68. I bambini devono rispondere del vetro rotto. 69. Lei deve rispondere delle sue azioni.

**scrivere**

70. Come si scrive il tuo cognome? 71. Devo scrivere a macchina la lettera? 72. Lei ha scritto al consolato italiano. 73. Dante ha scritto molto nella sua vita. 74. Lei spera che le scriverai presto. 75. Gli ho scritto di non venire.

**tenere**

76. Il bambino teneva in mano un giocattolo. 77. La polizia teneva in dietro la gente. 78. Ho tenuto l'acqua nel frigorifero. 79. Posso tenere il cappotto? Ho freddo. 80. Lei vuole tenere le finestre chiuse.

**vedere**

81. Hai visto un bel film? 82. Vorrei vederlo felice. 83. Non vedo l'ora di partire per l'Italia. 84. Si vede ancora la macchia? 85. Abbiamo visto una stella cadente. 86. Lui andrà a vedere sua mamma. 87. Loro andavano a vederlo sciare.

**vendere**

88. Lui vende libri. 89. Lei ha venduto molte case. 90. Loro vendono all'ingrosso. 91. Non mi piace vendere.

**volere**

92. Loro vorrebbero viaggiare, ma non possono. 93. Oggi, la mia macchina non vuole funzionare. 94. Lei non vuole che tu venga domani. 95. Vorrei (che) tu glielo dicessi. 96. Lei vuole studiare l'italiano. 97. Vogliamo vedere i tuoi quadri. 98. Lui vuole comprare una macchina nuova.

## Page 145, -ire Verbs

**aprire**

1. Apri la porta, per favore. 2. Vuole aprire un conto corrente. 3. Non aprire la televisione. 4. La banda apriva la parata.

**aprirsi**

5. I fiori primaverili si sono aperti. 6. La finestra dell'appartamento si apre sul mare. 7. La scuola si apre in autunno.

**costruire**

8. Stanno costruendo una nuova autostrada. 9. Spero di costruire una casa nuova. 10. Con molto lavoro, ti puoi costruire una fortuna.

**dire**

11. I bambini dicono spesso le bugie. 12. Suo padre glielo aveva detto. 13. Lei gli ha detto di chiamarci quando arrivano. 14. Spero (che) tu non abbia detto niente. 15. Digli la verità. 16. Il testimone ha detto che non aveva visto l'incidente.

**divertire**

17. I cartoni animati divertono i bambini. 18. La donna si diverte con i bambini.

**divertirsi**

19. Ti sei divertito a New York? 20. Divertiti! 21. Il bambino si diverte a giocare con i Legos. 22. Io al circo non mi diverto.

**finire**

23. Io so già come finisce il libro. 24. La lezione finisce alle 9:00 di sera. 25. Hai finito? 26. Hai finito tutti i soldi? 27. Il gelato è finito. 28. Non ho finito i miei compiti.

**partire**

29. Sono partiti per l'Italia in aereo. 30. I miei amici sono partiti ieri per la spiaggia. 31. Il treno parte alle 10:00 esatte. 32. Io partirò martedì. 33. Sono partiti presto.

**preferire**

34. Mia madre preferisce il caffè al tè. 35. Io preferisco più leggere che guardare la televisione. 36. Preferisco che tu stia dentro. 37. Preferiscono più sciare che pattinare.

**pulire**

38. Ogni venerdì io pulisco la casa. 39. Pulisci le scarpe prima di entrare. 40. Pulisciti il naso.

**salire**

41. La nave spaziale saliva molto velocemente. 42. Devi salire al terzo piano. 43. Il prezzo della frutta è salito ancora. 44. Deve salire sull'autobus. 45. Mia figlia è salita con l'ascensore.

**sentire**

46. La madre ha sentito il bambino piangere. 47. Hai sentito il concerto? 48. Vorrei sentire la tua opinione. 49. Mio nonno non sente bene.

**soffrire**

50. Giovanna soffre di mal di testa. 51. Soffrono di fame. 52. Gli alberi di arancio hanno sofferto per il gelo.

**spedire**

53. Ti spedirò una lettera. 54. Ti hanno spedito una scatola grande. 55. Vorrei spedirti un regalo.

**uscire**

56. Tuo padre è uscito a piedi. 57. I miei amici sono usciti mezz'ora fa. 58. Non uscire, piove.

**venire**

59. Vorresti venire con noi? 60. Sono venuti in Italia tanti anni fa. 61. Penso (che) stia venendo qualcuno. 62. A che ora sei venuto a casa? 63. Da dove viene quella ragazza? 64. Questo olio viene dalla fattoria. 65. La neve veniva giù lentamente.

# Verb Charts

## Regular Verbs

### Verbs Ending in *-are*

*Parlare*

**Present Indicative**
parlo, parli, parla, parliamo,
parlate, parlano

**Imperfect**
parlavo, parlavi, parlava,
parlavamo, parlavate, parlavano

**Future**
parlerò, parlerai, parlerà,
parleremo, parlerete, parleranno

**Imperative**
parla, parliamo, parlate
parli (pol. s.), parlino (pol pl.)

**Passato Remoto (Preterite)**
parlai, parlasti, parlò,
parlammo, parlaste, parlarono

**Passato Prossimo (Present Perfect)**
ho parlato, hai parlato, ha parlato,
abbiamo parlato, avete parlato,
hanno parlato

### Verbs Ending in *-ere*

*Perdere*

perdo, perdi, perde, perdiamo,
perdete, perdono

perdevo, perdevi, perdeva,
perdevamo, perdevate, perdevano

perderò, perderai, perderà,
perderemo, perderete, perderanno

perdi, perdiamo, perdete
perda (pol. s.), perdano (pol. pl.)

perdei, perdesti, perdè,
perdemmo, perdeste, perderono

ho perduto, hai perduto, ha perduto,
abbiamo perduto, avete perduto,
hanno perduto

## Parlare

### Trapassato Prossimo (Pluperfect)
*avevo parlato, avevi parlato,*
*aveva parlato, avevamo parlato,*
*avevate parlato, avevano parlato*

### Present Conditional
*parlerei, parleresti, parlerebbe,*
*parleremmo, parlereste, parlerebbero*

### Past Conditional
*avrei parlato, avresti parlato,*
*avrebbe parlato, avremmo parlato,*
*avreste parlato, avrebbero parlato*

### Present Subjunctive
*che io parli, tu parli, lui/lei parli,*
*noi parliamo, voi parliate,*
*loro parlino*

### Imperfect Subjunctive
*che io parlassi, tu parlassi,*
*lui/lei parlasse, noi parlassimo,*
*voi parlaste, loro parlassero*

### Past Subjunctive
*che io abbia parlato, tu abbia*
*parlato, lui/lei abbia parlato,*
*noi abbiamo parlato, voi abbiate*
*parlato, loro abbiano parlato*

### Pluperfect Subjunctive
*che io avessi parlato, tu avessi*
*parlato, lui/lei avesse parlato,*
*noi avessimo parlato, voi aveste*
*parlato, loro avessero parlato*

## Perdere

*avevo perduto, avevi perduto,*
*aveva perduto, avevamo perduto,*
*avevate perduto, avevano perduto*

*perderei, perderesti, perderebbe,*
*perderemmo, perdereste, perderebbero*

*avrei perduto, avresti perduto,*
*avrebbe perduto, avremmo perduto,*
*avreste perduto, avrebbero perduto*

*che io perda, tu perda, lui/lei perda,*
*noi perdiamo, voi perdiate,*
*loro perdano*

*che io perdessi, tu perdessi,*
*lui/lei perdesse, noi perdessimo,*
*voi perdeste, loro perdessero*

*che io abbia perduto, tu abbia*
*perduto, lui/lei abbia perduto,*
*noi abbiamo perduto, voi abbiate*
*perduto, loro abbiano perduto*

*che io avessi perduto, tu avessi*
*perduto, lui/lei avesse perduto,*
*noi avessimo perduto, voi aveste*
*perduto, loro avessero perduto*

# Verbs Ending in -ire

## Dormire

### Present Indicative
dormo, dormi, dorme, dormiamo,
dormite, dormono

### Imperfect
dormivo, dormivi, dormiva
dormivamo, dormivate, dormivano

### Future
dormirò, dormirai, dormirà,
dormiremo, dormirete, dormiranno

### Imperative
dormi, dormiamo, dormite
dorma (pol. s), dormano (pol. pl.)

### Passato Remoto (Preterite)
dormii, dormisti, dormì, dormimmo,
dormiste, dormirono

### Passato Prossimo (Present Perfect)
ho dormito, hai dormito, ha dormito,
abbiamo dormito, avete dormito,
hanno dormito

### Trapassato Prossimo (Pluperfect)
avevo dormito, avevi dormito,
aveva dormito, avevamo dormito,
avevate dormito, avevano dormito

# Verbs Ending in -ire (with isc)

## Finire

finisco, finisci, finisce, finiamo,
finite, finiscono

finivo, finivi, finiva,
finivamo, finivate, finivano

finirò, finirai, finirà,
finiremo, finirete, finiranno

finisci, finiamo, finite
finisca (pol. s.), finiscano (pol. pl.)

finii, finisti, finì, finimmo,
finiste, finirono

ho finito, hai finito, ha finito,
abbiamo finito, avete finito,
hanno finito

avevo finito, avevi finito,
aveva finito, avevamo finito,
avevate finito, avevano finito

| *Dormire* | *Finire* |
|---|---|

### *Present Conditional*

dormirei, dormiresti, dormirebbe,
dormiremmo, dormireste, dormirebbero

finirei, finiresti, finirebbe,
finiremmo, finireste, finirebbero

### *Past Conditional*

avrei dormito, avresti dormito,
avrebbe dormito, avremmo dormito,
avreste dormito, avrebbero dormito

avrei finito, avresti finito,
avrebbe finito, avremmo finito,
avreste finito, avrebbero finito

### *Present Subjunctive*

che io dorma, tu dorma, lui/lei dorma,
noi dormiamo, voi dormiate,
loro dormano

che io finisca, tu finisca, lui/lei finisca,
noi finiamo, voi finiate,
loro finiscano

### *Imperfect Subjunctive*

che io dormissi, tu dormissi,
lui/lei dormisse, noi dormissimo,
voi dormiste, loro dormissero

che io finissi, tu finissi,
lui/lei finisse, noi finissimo,
voi finiste, loro finissero

### *Past Subjunctive*

che io abbia dormito, tu abbia
dormito, lui/lei abbia dormito,
noi abbiamo dormito, voi abbiate
dormito, loro abbiano dormito

che io abbia finito, tu abbia
finito, lui/lei abbia finito,
noi abbiamo finito, voi abbiate
finito, loro abbiano finito

### *Pluperfect Subjunctive*

che io avessi dormito, tu avessi
dormito, lui/lei avesse dormito,
noi avessimo dormito, voi aveste
dormito, loro avessero dormito

che io avessi finito, tu avessi
finito, lui/lei avesse finito,
noi avessimo finito, voi aveste
finito, loro avessero finito

# Common Irregular Verbs

| *Fare* | *Dare* |
|---|---|

**Present Indicative**

faccio, fai, fa, facciamo,
fate, fanno

do, dai, dà, diamo, date, danno

**Imperfect**

facevo, facevi, faceva,
facevamo, facevate, facevano

davo, davi, dava, davamo,
davate, davano

**Future**

farò, farai, farà, faremo,
farete, faranno

darò, darai, darà, daremo,
darete, daranno

**Imperative**

fà (non fare), facciamo, fate
faccia (pol. s.), facciano (pol. pl.)

dà (non dare), diamo, date
dia (pol. s.), diano (pol. pl.)

**Passato Remoto (Preterite)**

feci, facesti, fece, facemmo,
faceste, facero

diedi, desti, diede, demmo,
deste, diedero

**Passato Prossimo (Present Perfect)**

ho fatto, hai fatto, ha fatto,
abbiamo fatto, avete fatto,
hanno fatto

ho dato, hai dato, ha dato,
abbiamo dato, avete dato,
hanno dato

**Trapassato Prossimo (Pluperfect)**

avevo fatto, avevi fatto,
aveva fatto, avevamo fatto,
avevate fatto, avevano fatto

avevo dato, avevi dato,
aveva dato, avevamo dato,
avevate dato, avevano dato

## Fare

**Present Conditional**
farei, faresti, farebbe,
faremmo, fareste, farebbero

**Past Conditional**
avrei fatto, avresti fatto,
avrebbe fatto, avremmo fatto,
avreste fatto, avrebbero fatto

**Present Subjunctive**
che io faccia, tu faccia, lui/lei faccia,
noi facciamo, voi facciate,
loro facciano

**Imperfect Subjunctive**
che io facessi, tu facessi,
lui/lei facesse, noi facessimo,
voi faceste, loro facessero

**Past Subjunctive**
che io abbia fatto, tu abbia
fatto, lui/lei abbia fatto,
noi abbiamo fatto, voi abbiate
fatto, loro abbiano fatto

**Pluperfect Subjunctive**
che io avessi fatto, tu avessi
fatto, lui/lei avesse fatto,
noi avessimo fatto, voi aveste
fatto, loro avessero fatto

## Dare

darei, daresti, darebbe,
daremmo, dareste, darebbero

avrei dato, avresti dato,
avrebbe dato, avremmo dato,
avreste dato, avrebbero dato

che io dia, tu dia, lui/lei dia,
noi diamo, voi diate,
loro diano

che io dessi, tu dessi,
lui/lei desse, noi dessimo,
voi deste, loro dessero

che io abbia dato, tu abbia
dato, lui/lei abbia dato,
noi abbiamo dato, voi abbiate
dato, loro abbiano dato

che io avessi dato, tu avessi
dato, lui/lei avesse dato,
noi avessimo dato, voi aveste
dato, loro avessero dato

## Vedere

### Present Indicative
vedo, vedi, vede, vediamo,
vedete, vedono

### Imperfect
vedevo, vedevi, vedeva,
vedevamo, vedevate, vedevano

### Future
vedrò, vedrai, vedrà, vedremo,
vedrete, vedranno

### Imperative
vedi (non vedere), vediamo, vedete
veda (pol. s.), vedano (pol. pl.)

### Passato Remoto (Preterite)
vidi, vedesti, vide, vedemmo,
vedeste, videro

### Passato Prossimo (Present Perfect)
ho visto, hai visto, ha visto,
abbiamo visto, avete visto,
hanno visto

### Trapassato Prossimo (Pluperfect)
avevo visto, avevi visto,
aveva visto, avevamo visto,
avevate visto, avevano visto

## Venire

### Present Indicative
vengo, vieni, viene, veniamo,
venite, vengono

### Imperfect
venivo, venivi, veniva, venivamo,
venivate, venivano

### Future
verrò, verrai, verrà, verremo,
verrete, verranno

### Imperative
vieni (non venire), veniamo, venite
venga (pol. s.), vengano (pol. pl.)

### Passato Remoto (Preterite)
venni, venisti, venne, venimmo,
veniste, vennero

### Passato Prossimo (Present Perfect)
sono venuto/a, sei venuto/a,
lui/lei è venuto/a, noi siamo venuti/e,
voi siete venuti/e, loro sono venuti/e

### Trapassato Prossimo (Pluperfect)
ero venuto/a, eri venuto/a,
era venuto/a, eravamo venuti/e,
eravate venuti/e, erano venuti/e

## Vedere

**Present Conditional**
vedrei, vedresti, vedrebbe,
vedremmo, vedreste, vedrebbero

**Past Conditional**
avrei visto, avresti visto,
avrebbe visto, avremmo visto,
avreste visto, avrebbero visto

**Present Subjunctive**
che io veda, tu veda, lui/lei veda,
noi vediamo, voi vediate,
loro vedano

**Imperfect Subjunctive**
che io vedessi, tu vedessi,
lui/lei vedesse, noi vedessimo,
voi vedeste, loro vedessero

**Past Subjunctive**
che io abbia visto, tu abbia
visto, lui/lei abbia visto,
noi abbiamo visto, voi abbiate
visto, loro abbiano visto

**Pluperfect Subjunctive**
che io avessi visto, tu avessi
visto, lui/lei avesse visto,
noi avessimo visto, voi aveste
visto, loro avessero visto

## Venire

**Present Conditional**
verrei, verresti, verrebbe,
verremmo, verreste, verrebbero

**Past Conditional**
sarei venuto/a, saresti venuto/a,
sarebbe venuto/a, saremmo venuti/e,
sareste venuti/e, sarebbero venuti/e

**Present Subjunctive**
che io venga, tu venga, lui/lei venga,
noi veniamo, voi veniate,
loro vengano

**Imperfect Subjunctive**
che io venissi, tu venissi,
lui/lei venisse, noi venissimo,
voi veniste, loro venissero

**Past Subjunctive**
che io sia venuto/a, tu sia
venuto/a, lui/lei sia venuto/a,
noi siamo venuti/e, voi siate
venuti/e, loro siano venuti/e

**Pluperfect Subjunctive**
che io fossi venuto/a, tu fossi venuto/a,
lui/lei fosse venuto/a,
noi fossimo venuti/e, voi foste venuti/e,
loro fossero venuti/e

# Index of Verbs

## Italian–English

### A

**abitare**   to live
**accadere**   to happen
**accedere**   to access
**accendere**   to light
**accettare**   to accept
**acconsentire**   to agree
**aderire**   to adhere
**aggiungere**   to add
**aiutare**   to help
**alzarsi**   to get up
**amare**   to love
**andare**   to go
**apparire**   to appear
**appendere**   to hang
**applaudire**   to applaud
**apprendere**   to learn
**aprire**   to open
**arrestare**   to arrest
**arrivare**   to arrive
**ascoltare**   to listen
**aspettare**   to wait
**assentire**   to consent
**assistere**   to assist
**assolvere**   to absolve
**assumere**   to assume, hire
**attendere**   to attend
**attribuire**   to attribute
**avere**   to have
**avvenire**   to happen
**avvertire**   to announce

### B

**ballare**   to dance
**bere**   to drink
**benedire**   to bless
**bollire**   to boil

### C

**cadere**   to fall
**cambiare**   to change
**camminare**   to walk
**cantare**   to sing
**capire**   to understand
**cenare**   to have supper
**chiedere**   to ask
**chiudere**   to close
**cogliere**   to gather
**colpire**   to hit
**cominciare**   to start
**comprare**   to buy
**comprendere**   to comprehend
**concludere**   to conclude
**condividere**   to share
**confondere**   to confuse
**conoscere**   to know
**consentire**   to agree
**conseguire**   to result
**consistere**   to consist
**contare**   to count
**controllare**   to control
**convertire**   to convert
**convincere**   to convince
**coprire**   to cover
**correggere**   to correct
**correre**   to run
**costruire**   to build
**credere**   to believe
**crescere**   to grow
**cucire**   to sew
**cuocere**   to cook

### D

**dare**   to give
**decidere**   to decide
**desiderare**   to wish
**difendere**   to defend
**digerire**   to digest
**dimagrire**   to lose weight

**dimenticare**   to forget
**dire**   to tell, say
**dirigere**   to direct
**discutere**   to discuss
**distinguere**   to distinguish
**diventare**   to become
**divertire**   to enjoy
**dividere**   to divide
**domandare**   to ask
**donare**   to donate
**dormire**   to sleep
**dovere**   must

# E

**eleggere**   to elect
**entrare**   to enter
**esaminare**   to examine
**esaurire**   to exhaust
**esibire**   to exhibit
**esistere**   to exist
**esprimere**   to express
**essere**   to be

# F

**fallire**   to fail
**fare**   to do, make
**fermare**   to stop
**ferire**   to wound
**finire**   to finish
**firmare**   to sign
**fuggire**   to escape

# G

**garantire**   to guarantee
**gestire**   to manage
**giocare**   to play
**girare**   to turn
**godere**   to enjoy
**guardare**   to look
**guarire**   to heal
**guidare**   to drive
**gustare**   to taste

# I

**illustrare**   to illustrate
**imparare**   to learn
**includere**   to include
**inghiottire**   to swallow
**insegnare**   to teach
**inseguire**   to follow, chase
**insistere**   to insist
**interrompere**   to interrupt
**investire**   to invest
**ispezionare**   to inspect
**istruire**   to instruct
**invadere**   to invade
**invitare**   to invite

# L

**lasciare**   to leave
**lavare**   to wash
**lavorare**   to work
**leggere**   to read
**litigare**   to quarrel

# M

**mandare**   to send
**mangiare**   to eat
**mentire**   to lie
**mettere**   to put
**morire**   to die
**mostrare**   to show
**muovere**   to move

# N

**nascere**   to be born
**nascondere**   to hide
**nevicare**   to snow
**notare**   to notice
**nuotare**   to swim

# O

**offrire**   to offer
**organizzare**   to organize

# P

**pagare**   to pay
**parlare**   to speak, talk

**partire**   to leave, depart
**pensare**   to think
**perdere**   to lose
**perdonare**   to forgive
**permettere**   to allow
**piangere**   to cry
**piantare**   to plant
**piovere**   to rain
**porre**   to put
**portare**   to bring
**potere**   to be able
**pranzare**   to dine
**preferire**   to prefer
**prendere**   to take
**pretendere**   to pretend
**prevenire**   to prevent
**promettere**   to promise
**promuovere**   to promote
**proporre**   to propose
**proteggere**   to protect
**provare**   to try
**provvedere**   to provide
**pulire**   to clean
**punire**   to punish

## R

**raccontare**   to narrate
**raggiungere**   to reach
**rallentare**   to slow down
**regalare**   to give a gift, donate
**restare**   to stay
**restituire**   to return
**ricevere**   to receive
**richiedere**   to request
**ricordare**   to remember
**ridere**   to laugh
**ridurre**   to reduce
**rimanere**   to remain
**rimuovere**   to remove
**riposare**   to rest
**risolvere**   to resolve
**rispondere**   to answer
**ritornare**   to return
**riunire**   to reunite
**rompere**   to break

## S

**salire**   to climb
**saltare**   to jump
**sapere**   to know
**scegliere**   to choose
**scendere**   to descend
**sciare**   to ski
**scomparire**   to disappear
**scoprire**   to discover
**scrivere**   to write
**seguire**   to follow
**sentire**   to hear
**seppellire**   to bury
**servire**   to serve
**soffrire**   to suffer
**sognare**   to dream
**sorridere**   to smile
**sostituire**   to substitute
**spedire**   to send
**spegnere**   to turn off
**spendere**   to spend
**sperare**   to hope
**spiegare**   to explain
**spingere**   to push
**stabilire**   to establish
**stare**   to stay
**stirare**   to iron
**studiare**   to study
**succedere**   to happen
**suggerire**   to suggest
**suonare**   to play
**svegliare**   to wake up
**svenire**   to faint

## T

**tagliare**   to cut
**telefonare**   to telephone
**temere**   to fear
**tenere**   to keep
**togliere**   to remove
**tornare**   to return
**tradire**   to betray
**tradurre**   to translate
**trasferire**   to transfer
**trasmettere**   to broadcast
**trovare**   to find

## U

**ubbidire**   to obey
**udire**   to hear
**unire**   to unite
**urlare**   to scream
**uscire**   to go out

## V

**valere**   to be worth
**vedere**   to see

**vendere**   to sell
**venire**   to come
**vestire**   to dress
**viaggiare**   to travel
**vincere**   to win
**visitare**   to visit
**vivere**   to live
**volare**   to fly
**volere**   to want
**votare**   to vote

# Index of Verbs

## English–Italian

### A

absolve **assolvere**
accept **accettare**
access **accedere**
add **aggiungere**
adhere **aderire**
agree **acconsentire**
answer **rispondere**
appear **apparire**
applaud **applaudire**
arrest **arrestare**
arrive **arrivare**
ask **chiedere**
assist **assistere**
assume **assumere**
attend **attendere**
attribute **attribuire**

### B

be **essere**
be born **nascere**
become **diventare, divenire**
believe **credere**
betray **tradire**
bless **benedire**
blow up **gonfiare**
boil **bollire**
break **rompere**
bring **portare**
build **costruire**
bury **seppellire**
buy **comprare**

### C

call **chiamare**
can **potere**
cancel **cancellare**
change **cambiare**
choose **scegliere**
clean **pulire**
climb **salire**
close **chiudere**
come **venire**
complete **completare**
comprehend **comprendere**
conclude **concludere**
confuse **confondere**
consent **consentire**
control **controllare**
convert **convertire**
convince **convincere**
cook **cuocere**
correct **correggere**
count **contare**
cover **coprire**
cry **piangere**
cut **tagliare**

### D

dance **ballare**
decide **decidere**
defend **difendere**
define **definire**
depart **partire**
descend **scendere**
die **morire**
digest **digerire**
dine **cenare**
direct **dirigere**
disappear **sparire**
discover **scoprire**
discuss **discutere**
distinguish **distinguere**
divide **dividere**
do **fare**
donate **donare**
dream **sognare**
dress **vestire**
drink **bere**

## E

eat **mangiare**
elect **eleggere**
enjoy **godere**
enter **entrare**
escape **fuggire**
establish **stabilire**
examine **esaminare**
exhaust **esaurire**
exhibit **esibire**
exist **esistere**
expire **scadere**
explain **spiegare**
express **esprimere**

## F

fail **fallire**
fall **cadere**
fear **temere**
feed **nutrire**
find **trovare**
finish **finire**
flee **scappare**
fly **volare**
follow **seguire**
forget **dimenticare**
forgive **perdonare**

## G

gather **raccogliere**
get up **alzarsi**
give up **arrendersi**
give **dare**
give a gift **regalare**
go **andare**
go crazy **impazzire**
go out **uscire**
grow **crescere**
guarantee **garantire**

## H

hang **appendere**
happen **accadere**
have **avere**
heal **guarire**

hear **sentire, udire**
help **aiutare**
hide **nascondere**
hope **sperare**

## I

illustrate **illustrare**
include **includere**
insert **inserire**
insist **insistere**
inspect **ispezionare**
install **installare**
instruct **istruire**
interrupt **interrompere**
invite **invitare**

## J

jump **saltare**

## K

keep **tenere**
know (something) **sapere**
know (somebody) **conoscere**

## L

laugh **ridere**
learn **imparare**
leave **lasciare, partire**
lie **mentire**
listen **ascoltare**
live **vivere**
look **guardare**
lose **perdere**
lose weight **dimagrire**
love **amare**

## M

make **fare**
move **muovere**
must **dovere**

## N

notify **avvertire**

## O

obey **obbedire**
offer **offrire**
organize **organizzare**

## P

paint **dipingere**
pay **pagare**
permit **permettere**
plant **piantare**
play **giocare, suonare**
prefer **preferire**
pretend **pretendere**
prevent **prevenire**
proceed **procedere**
promise **promettere**
propose **proporre**
protect **proteggere**
provide **provvedere**
punish **punire**
put **mettere**

## R

rain **piovere**
reach **raggiungere**
read **leggere**
receive **ricevere**
reduce **ridurre**
remain **rimanere**
remember **ricordare**
remove **spostare**
request **richiedere**
resolve **risolvere**
rest **riposare**
result **conseguire**
return **ritornare, tornare**
reunite **riunire**
run **correre**

## S

say **dire**
scream **urlare**
see **vedere**

sell **vendere**
send **mandare**
serve **servire**
sew **cucire**
share **condividere**
show **mostrare**
sign **firmare**
sing **cantare**
ski **sciare**
sleep **dormire**
slow down **rallentare**
smile **sorridere**
snow **nevicare**
speak **parlare**
spend **spendere**
start **cominciare**
stay **stare**
stop **fermare**
study **studiare**
substitute **sostituire**
succeed **avere successo**
suffer **soffrire**
swallow **inghiottire**
swim **nuotare**

## T

take **prendere**
take off **partire**
taste **assaggiare, gustare**
teach **insegnare**
tell **dire**
think **pensare**
transfer **trasferire**
translate **tradurre**
transmit **trasmettere**
travel **viaggiare**
try **provare**
turn **girare**
turn off **spegnere**

## U

understand **capire**
unite **unire**

## V

visit **visitare**
vote **votare**

## W

wait **aspettare**
walk **camminare**
wash **lavare**
wish **desiderare**
work **lavorare**
write **scrivere**